WINGS OF HOPE

WINGS OF HOPE

A JOURNEY OF INSPIRATIONAL POEMS AND SONGS

JEAN ANN ROBINSON

CITIOFBOOKS, INC.
3736 Eubank NE Suite A1
Albuquerque, NM 87111-3579
www.citiofbooks.com

Hotline: 1 (877) 389-2759
Fax: 1 (505) 930-7244

Ordering Information:

Quantity sales. Special discounts are available on quantity purchases by corporations, associations, and others. For details, contact the publisher at the address above.

Printed in the United States of America.

ISBN-13:   Softcover   979-8-90124-436-4
               eBook   979-8-90124-437-1

Library of Congress Control Number: 2026909940

TABLE OF CONTENTS

"Awaken Your Strength"

In the depths of night, where shadows play,
A spark ignites to light your way.
With every stumble, rise and soar,
Your heart beats fiercely, forevermore.

Let worries fade like morning mist,
Embrace each challenge, persist, persist.
For within your mind, a wisdom untold,
A treasure of courage, brave and bold.

Nurture your soul, let kindness flow,
In acts of love, your spirit will grow.
Strengthen your heart with hope's warm embrace,
Embody the light, shine with grace.

Through trials faced, you will become,
A symphony of strength, a beating drum.
So rise, dear friend, let fears take flight,
For you are the fire that conquers the night.

"Beacon of Light"

In the shadow's grip. I stand so tall,
A beacon of positivity, guiding through all.
With every sunrise, my spirit ignites,
Chasing away darkness, spreading the lights.

Through storms and troubles, I'll shine bright,
Whispers of hope in the depths of the night.
With laughter and in kindness, I pave the way,
Transforming the clouds into joys of the day.

Together we'll rise, hand in hand we'll climb,
In a world that seems heavy, let's dance with time.
For I am a beacon, steadfast and true,
A spark of inspiration, igniting in you.

"Cradled in Divine Hands"

In the quiet moments of my day,
When shadows cast their fleeting sway,
I feel a presence, calm and grand,
For God has made me in His gentle hand.
Through stormy seas and skies of gray,
A guiding light, He paves my way.
His love, a shield, forever stands,
For I am cradled in God's divine hands.
When doubts arise, and fears expand,
He lifts me high, helps me withstand.
With every heartbeat, I'm reassured,
By the strength of his grip, I'm secured.
In joys and trials, tears and glee,
His promise holds, steadfast and free.
Embraced by grace, forever planned,
God keeps me safe in His caring hand.
So I walk with faith, heart untrammeled,
Through life's journey, graceless yet
unshackled.
With trust in His eternal bands,
Knowing I'm held in the palm of His hands.

"From the Depths, We Rise"

We've walked through the shadows, scorched and scarred,
In the furnace of life, we fought hard, battled hard,
From the depths of hell, we found our way,
Guided by hope, we rise each day.
Our journey's toll, etched deep in our soul,
A journey of survival, a hard-won goal,
We carry the scars, but not the despair—
For in every wound, there's a strength rare.
We have a duty, a sacred call,
To lift our children, to raise them all,
Not just our blood, but every child's face,
To heal their wounds, to give them grace.
Let's plant in their hearts the seeds of
God's love,
A guide, a light, to rise above,
To fill their spirit with peace and joy,
To cherish each girl, each boy.
For they are the future, hope's bright flame,
On their wings, we must stake our claim,
To love, to nurture, to prepare the way—
So they may thrive and never stray.
From the ashes of our pain, we now see—
Our mission is boundless, our destiny—free,
To carry the torch, to lead, to heal,

To ensure they flourish with love's true seal.
Together we stand, resilient and strong,
In this sacred duty, we belong,
From the depths, we rise, and in unity,
We forge a future of hope and mercy.

"Guided by Higher Values"

In the dawn's soft light, I find my way,
A path of honor where I choose to stay.
With every choice, my heart's desire,
Awakens the soul, ignites the fire.
Through trials faced and mountain steep,
I hold my value close, their promises I keep.
Integrity whispers in the darkest night,
Guiding my spirit to what is right.

"Harmony's Dawn"

In the quiet hush of dawn's first light,
Where shadows fade and hopes ignite,
A whisper spreads across the sky,
A call for love that never dies.
From every mountain, every shore,
A symphony of hearts roars,
Bridging divides, mending the seams,
Uniting souls with shared dreams.
Let kindness be our guiding star,
Turning wounds to healing scars,
For in unity we find,
A peace that's boundless, free, and kind.
Raise your voice in gentle song,
In the world where we belong,
Salvation blooms within each heart,
A world reborn, a brand-new start.
Together we forge a shining way,
Building tomorrow on love's pure ray,
A legacy of hope, of grace,
Eternal love, embracing every place.
Oh, let love be the victory,
Peace and joy for all to see,
Salvation's call, in every heart,
A brand new world, a fresh new start.

"Radiant Beacon"

In the depth of daunting shadows, I arise,
A vibrant light beneath vast, open skies.
With every breath, I gather the dawn,
A tapestry woven, a new day reborn.
I stand as a lighthouse, steadfast and true,
Guiding lost souls with a warmth that
breaks through.

With whispers of hope, like a gentle wave crest,
I share the calm strength that dwells in
my chest.

Through storms of despair, where darkness
may roam,
I shine with assurance, inviting them home.
For in the ember of my radiant glow,
Together, we flourish, together, we grow.
Each spark I ignited was a reflection of love,
A reminder of strength from the heavens above.
I am a beacon, a flame bright and free,
Radiating resilience, for all who can see.

"Resilience Amidst the Shifting Sands"

In the vast and restless desert of dreams,
Where intentions drift like fleeting streams,
Stand firm, O soul, amidst the whirl,
A steadfast heart begins to unfurl.
The world is a mirror, ever-changing face,
Lies intertwined in hidden grace,
With every gust of shifting wind,
A beginning to rescind or mend.
Through storms of doubt and waves of fear,
Find the voice that calls you near,
For in the chaos, seeds are sown,
Strength in struggles, growth is grown.
Remember, stones may tumble, rivers bend,
Yet inner fire can transcend, defend,
A resilient mind, a spirit bold,
Can turn the coldest night to gold.
Adapt, evolve, and embrace the flow,
Like rivers that eternally go,
For survival, art is to persist,
In a world of twisters and mists.
So rise anew with each dawn's light,
Guided by hope and inner might,
In shifting sands, stand tall, be free—
A beacon of resilience, eternally.

In every heartbeat, a whisper vow,
To rise again, despite the how,
For every fall and every tear,
Build the strength to preserve.

The sky may darken, clouds may swirl,
Yet within lies an unyielding pearl,
A spark that refuses to fade away,
Illuminating each shadowed day.
Hold fast to purpose, cherish the core,
Let courage guide you to explore,
Uncharted paths and unknown heights,
Turning struggles into luminous lights.
For survival is not mere endurance,
But a dance with fate, a spirited dance,
Where hope blooms in the hardest soil,
And dreams ignite earnest toil.
So walk the road with fearless grace,
With love and hope etched on your face,
In shifting worlds, you'll find your tune—
A melody of strength, forever in bloom.
With every step upon uncertain ground,
A sacred purpose must be found,
To anchor heart in steadfast truth,
A guiding light amid the youth.
The winds of change may tear and bend.
But never break a soul that bends,
For within each challenge, lessons lie,
Lifting spirits to soar high.
Embrace the chaos, dance with the storm,
Find opportunity in the norm,
Transforming trails into strength anew,

A resilient spirit shining through.

Linger not on what once was lost,
But cherish all the world has tossed,
For every shadow cast by night,
Prepares you for the new dawning light.
In the face of shifting intentions guise,
Let your courage be your eternal prize,
A beacon bright and fiercely true—
Survivor's soul, forever new.

"Stand, One More Dawn"

Stand, one more dawn – the night gives way,
A heartbeat steady, small but brave.
You are not a shadow, you are the day that
finds its shape with every wave.
There are hands you haven't met
yet, still, stories waiting in your name.
The road's rough, no matter who you are;
and that pain does not define your flame.
Breathe slowly — so the world can listen
when you speak the truth, you hide inside.
Courage shows up in quiet things:
A step, a call, a call, a moment tried.
Remember how a seed survives
beneath the weight of winter's lie;
it learns to keep its secret life
until the sun decides to rise.
You're more than every broken line,
more than the dark that edged your past.
Hope isn't loud — it's patient work,
a steady build that's meant to last.
Find one small reason, guard it close:
a friend, a song, a favorite place.
Hold on to that — it pulls you through,
it'll anchor you in time and space.

If you stumble, you know this truth:
a scar, a map of where you went.
Each marks a lesson, not an end –
A story stitched, a testament.

There's strength in asking for a hand,
in saying,

"I'm not fine today."

Pride will bend for what is real;
Realness grows the only way.
Stand, one more dawn — the light's not gone.
Your name belongs to future cheers. Walk on,
Not flawless but alive, and let tomorrow hold your years.
Listen — there are mornings made for you,
quiet gold that finds the street.
You'll meet new laughter, new mistakes, and learn how gentle victories
meet. Let anger be a teacher, not a chain;
Let sorrow shape your open hands.
Turn fear into a question: "What if...?" And let curiosity make plans.
Build small rituals that keep you whole — A walk, a line of verse, a call.
Celebrate the simple, stubborn wins: a surprise was watched, a problem
solved. Surround yourself with honest lights
— people who'll hear.
Trade the masks for accurate reflections;
real bonds repair what wear and tear. When nights get heavy, send a
thread into the world — a message, a plea. You may find strangers who will
hold you, or kin whose words become the key.
Imagine one day telling this: "I almost left, but chose to stay."
Your voice will help another later, a lamp passed on along the way.
So tend your edges with a steady hand, forgive the rush of youth's
mistakes. Hope grows slow, but roots run deep – and life rewards the soul
that wakes. Stand, one more dawn — keep tending light.
One step,... one breath,... one human try. You are a story not yet finished;
Live ... to see your own reply.

"Strength in Grace"

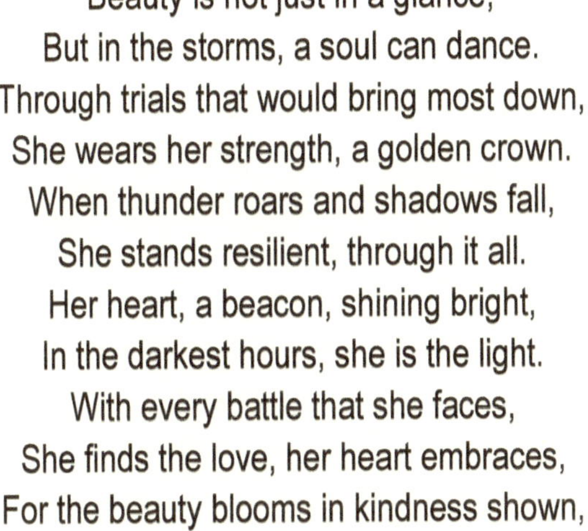

Beauty is not just in a glance,
But in the storms, a soul can dance.
Through trials that would bring most down,
She wears her strength, a golden crown.
When thunder roars and shadows fall,
She stands resilient, through it all.
Her heart, a beacon, shining bright,
In the darkest hours, she is the light.
With every battle that she faces,
She finds the love, her heart embraces,
For the beauty blooms in kindness shown,
In every hug and seed that's sown.
So when you see her gentle face,
Remember strength and love's embrace.
For true beauty, as we know,
It's how she carries storms and grows.

"The Embrace of Inner Calm"

In the quiet dawn of a restless mind,
Where shadows of doubt and fear often bind,
There blooms a truth, subtly deep, profound—
That peace in acceptance is truly found.
Like rivers that flow to reclaim their course,
Let go of resistance with gentle force,
For in surrender, a strength is revealed,
A tranquil heart, once fragile, now healed.
Acceptance is the gentle hand that soothes,
The inner voice that softly moves—
"All is as it is, and that is enough."
A tender whisper, a loving touch.
In embracing what we cannot control,
We feel the burden and soothe the soul,
Not resignation, but a wiser view,
To see life's ebb and flow anew.
Peace blossoms in this tender art,
A harmony rooted in the heart—
When we accept, we truly start
To live in love and not fall apart.
So let go of what you cannot change,
In acceptance, find your range,
A calm that deepens, a light so pure,
In peace, forever to endure.

"The Power Within: A Mind Unleashed"

In the silent chambers of the mind's vast domain,
Lies a spark of brilliance, a flicker beyond pain.
A sanctuary of thoughts, a restless, burning flame,
Waiting to be kindled, to ignite and proclaim.
A mind is a terrible thing to waste, they say,
For within its depths, dreams find their way.
Ideas like stars in the midnight sky,
Shining brightest when we dare to try.
It holds the power to heal, to build, to create,
To turn despair into hope, darkness into light's fate.
With each thought, a seed of change is sown,
A garden of potential, waiting to be grown.
Do not let fear or doubt drown your voice,
For each moment lost is a missed choice.
Embrace the challenge, the struggle, the fight,
For your mind is your weapon, your beacon of light.
Unleash the spirit that lies deep within,
Break free from the chains that hold you akin.
Rise above the shadows, let your mind soar,
For a terrible mind wasted is an eternity's bore.
So nurture your thoughts, let wisdom be your guide,
In the vastness of your mind, let your dreams reside.
A terrible thing it is to slip away,
The power of your mind — seize it today.

"The Sacred Embrace of a Good Woman"

In the quiet of dawn's gentle light,
Her love whispers, pure and bright.
A sacred flame that burns serene,
In her heart, a grace unseen.
Her kindness blooms like dawn's first rose,
In every touch, her mercy shows.
And guiding star in darkest night,
Her love a beacon, shining bright.
The strength she bears with tender grace,
A calm resilience etched on her face.
In her eyes, a universe divine,
A love so deep, so pure, so mine.
Her presence heals, her voice is balm,
A sacred trust, a steady Calm.
In her embrace, life finds its song,
A sacred love, forever strong.
Oh, blessed soul, so sacred, true,
In her love, I find anew—
A divine gift, a gentle grace,

The sacred love of a good woman's embrace.

"There Is No One Quite Like You"

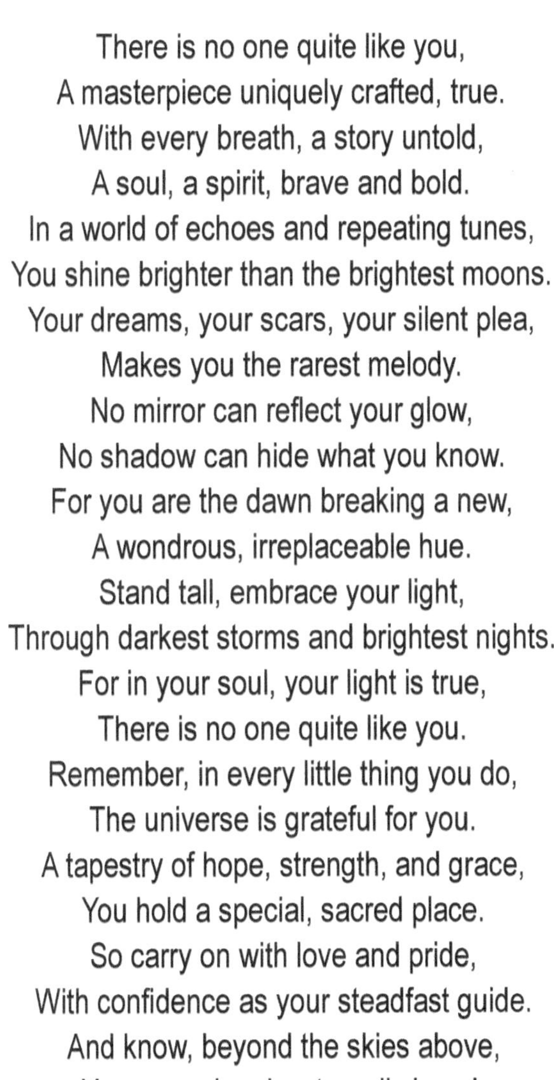

There is no one quite like you,
A masterpiece uniquely crafted, true.
With every breath, a story untold,
A soul, a spirit, brave and bold.
In a world of echoes and repeating tunes,
You shine brighter than the brightest moons.
Your dreams, your scars, your silent plea,
Makes you the rarest melody.
No mirror can reflect your glow,
No shadow can hide what you know.
For you are the dawn breaking a new,
A wondrous, irreplaceable hue.
Stand tall, embrace your light,
Through darkest storms and brightest nights.
For in your soul, your light is true,
There is no one quite like you.
Remember, in every little thing you do,
The universe is grateful for you.
A tapestry of hope, strength, and grace,
You hold a special, sacred place.
So carry on with love and pride,
With confidence as your steadfast guide.
And know, beyond the skies above,
You are uniquely, eternally loved.

"True North"

In a world of masks and fleeting lights,
Where shadows dance in dazzling sights,
The tide pulls hard, a relentless force,
Yet deep within, you chart your course.
To rise above the whispered doubt,
To hear your heart beyond the shout,
Is bravely standing on your own ground,
In authenticity, your strength is found.
The road may twist, the path may be steep,
But weave your truth, and the soul will leap.
For every moment that you embrace,
Your spirit shines, your rightful place.
So stand tall, let the world sway,
In the vibrant hues of your own array.
To be yourself—what a noble quest,
In being you lies the ultimate test.
In a realm of change, a rare delight,
Being yourself is the purest light.

"WORTHY"

She Paid Her Dues

In shadows deep where dreams may hide,
A fire burns bright, a fearless guide.
She rises bold, despite her scars,
A shining star beneath the scars.
Her journey long, through storm and strife,
Each step she took shaped her life.
With grit and grace, she fought the fight,
Turning darkness into light.
she's worthy of every dawn's embrace,
Of love, of hope, of boundless grace.
Her soul endured the hardest seeds,
For she knew, she paid her dues indeed.
No mountain high, no valley low,
It could stop her from having a steady flow.
Her strength is a testament to the truth, so true
A story that is written just for you.
Now stand in awe, in wonder's hue,
For all she's conquered, all she's grew.
She's worthy of her rightful place,
A champion of her own fierce grace.
Remember well, the roads she paved,
The fierce resilience she has saved.

For in her heart, she clearly sees,
Her worth was earned—her destiny.

A Beauty So Rare

In a world of fleeting shadows and shifting sand,
There shines a light that's truly grand,
A gentle glow, a tender grace ,
A beauty that none can quite replace.
With eyes that hold the dawn's first spark,
And a smile that brightens life's dark,
Her soul, a tapestry of hope,
A sacred song, a melody's scope.
Through storms she walks with quiet might,
A beacon in the endless night,
Reminding us of strength within,
The love, the courage, born from sin.
For in her rare and radiant air,
Blooms hope beyond compare,
A reminder that true beauty's rare,
Lies in the heart, deep and fair.
So cherish every moment, hold her near,
In her, the truest light appears,
A beauty so rare, forever to share,
A gift of love beyond compare.

A Black Woman Grace Is a Force Is a Sign

In the heart of a storm, she stand tall,
A beacon of strength, breaking every wall.
Her spirit, a river, deep and wide,
A force of resilience, with nothing to hide.
Her grace, a song in the silent night,
A sign of hope, of shining light.
In her eyes, stories of power and grace,
A mirror of past, present, future embrace.
She carries the world on her righteous shoulders,
Breaking barriers, as her story unfolds.
A testament that love truely can rise,
A black woman's soul, no disguise.
Her journey, a spark that ignites the sky,
An unyielding force, a reason why
We stand in awe, we stand in pride,
For she is the sign, the force, the guide.
In her grace we find our worth,
A testament to all her mirth.
A black woman, fierce and kind—
A force, a sign, forever designed.

A Chain Of Echoes

In twilight's gentle embrace, it gleams,
An emblem of whispers, of unspoken dreams.
Forged in the fires of trials once met,
This chain around my neck is a timeless duet.
Each linked moment, a story entwined,
A tapestry woven with memories confined.
It rests upon my heart, a silent decree,
Binding past and present, in unison with me.
Forged by the hands of fate's careful might,
Its weight is a reminder of shadows and light.
A circle unbroken, a journey begun,
Through corridors of time where the echoes run.

Adorned with reflections of battles I've fought,
In the silence, its presence was a comfort I sought.
With every heartbeat, its rhythm aligns,
A symphony played by the passage of time.
Beneath the surface, where secrets reside,
This chain speaks of love, of loss, and of pride.
Formal in nature, yet deeply it breathes,
A testament forged, as the spirit believes.
So let this chain linger, a guardian near,
In whispers of elegance, it conquers my fears.
For in every glimmer, a promise takes flight,
A chain around my neck, in the stillness of night.

A Force, A Sign

I'm a force, unyielding and true,
A windswept storm with a sky so blue,
Bearing the fire that fuel my soul,
A fearless heart that's whole.
I am a sign, a guiding light,
In the darkness, shining bright,
A whisper of hope in the stormy night.
A promise of dawn's first light.
Through struggles and tears, I stand tall,
A testament to the strength in us all.
With every fall, I rise anew,
Knowing my power is shining through.
I am a force, I am a sign,
A beacon of love, a voice divine,
Embracing my truth, wild and free,
This is who I am—endlessly me.

A Higher Reality

In the hush of dawn, where whispers reside,
Amidst the soft glow, where dreams gently glide,
There lies a truth in the morning's embrace,
A higher reality, a sacred place.
With each fluttering leaf, a story unfolds,
The tapestry woven, in colors of gold,
Each heartbeat is a rhythm, echoing grace,
In the stillness, we find our rightful space.
Look to the heavens, the stars gleam so bright,
They guide us through the darkness, a beacon of light,
With faith as our anchor, we reach for the sky,
In pursuit of the spirit, our soul learns to fly.
When trials around us, and shadows loom near,
Remember the promise: the dawn will be clear,
For every tear shed is a seed for the soul,
In the soil of our struggles, we discover our whole.
Together we rise when love lights the way,
Hand in hand through the night, into the day,
A dance of connection, a symphony grand,
In the heart of each other, we find where we stand.
So trust in the journey, the path yet untold,
In moments of silence, let courage unfold.
For within every heartbeat, there's more to reveal,
In the higher reality, we learn how to heal.

A message to Man

In the garden of life, you stand so tall,
A partner in love, answering the call.
Your woman, a flower, in need of the sun,
Together, you'll flourish. Two hearts beat as one.
She yearns for your knowing, your tender embrace,
To see her as she is, in her own sacred space.
Help her gently blossom, let her roots intertwine,
While nurturing her dreams, let her spirit forever shine.
In her heart lies a treasure, a world yet to see,
Your love can be magic, make her all she can be.
Together you're heroes, a tale to unfold,
A fairytale ending, with love pure as gold.
Through valleys and mountains, through laughter
and tears,
She hopes for more ups, to conquer her fears.
Remember each moment, both big and small,
Those "just because" days, they're the sweetest
of all.
Embrace every challenge, as partners in tune,
For love can be vibrant, like the dance of the moon.
So listen, dear man, to her heart's gentle hum,
For in knowing her fully, true happiness will come.
In the dance of forever, let your souls intertwine,
A journey together, where dreams brightly shine.

With patience and kindness, let love be your guide,
A message to man: take pride in her.

A Phenomenal Black woman,

I Walk with Grace, Move with Finesse
I stand tall amid the storm and rain,
A queen whose spirit breaks each chain,
With eyes that hold a universe's shine,
A heart that beat through every line.
I walk with grace, a silent song,
In a world that sometimes gets it wrong,
Finesse in every step I take,
A legacy no time can break.
Born from strength, woven with love,
A story written from dreams above,
Phenomenal in my own right,
A shining star within the night.
Voices may tremble, doubts may call,
But I rise, I stand, I give my all,
For I am more than they can see,
A Black woman, fierce and free.
Through every challenge, I remain,
A force of hope, a breaking chain,
With grace I walk, with faith I stride,
In my soul, pride and truth abide.
This is my time, my voice, my space,
A testament to love and grace,
For I am a queen, deeply blessed,
A phenomenal Black woman, at her best.

A Reflection of struggle

Look me in the eyes and tell me what you see,
A reflection, a soul longing to be free.
Eyes that have witnessed storms and silent despair,
Yet still hold the spark of hope burning bright and rare.
Do you see the fire that refuse to die,
The dreams that soar beyond the endless sky?
A heart that beats with unwavering might,
Fighting shadows to find the light.
In these depths, stories of battles fought alone,
Of courage unearthed, of strength I've known.
They tell of scars, both visible and and the unseen,
Stories of a rise from the in-between.
Look deeper, and you'll find the passion that roars,
A will to break down all the closed doors.
For within these eyes there's a fierce desire,
To reach higher, to inspire, to ignite the fire.
So ask yourself, what do you truly see?
A mirror of resilience, unbowed, and free.
And in that reflection, find your own way,
To face the darkness and bring forth the day.

A Woman Who Survived Her Storm

She walked through midnight with the sky split wide,
Collected shards of thunder, kept them inside;
Each step is a drumbeat carved from fear and flame.
She learned to speak the storm and not its name.
Rain tried to drown the rhythm of her feet,
Wind sought to teach her how despair could cheat.
Instead, she built a harbor from the pain,
A quiet harbor where her hope remains.
Scars like moon-maps glow upon her skin,
Reminders of the battles she lived in;
Not broken—tempered, forged by searing light,
A steel-born grace that dances in the night.
When dawn arrived, she offered hands and fire,
Transformed her wounds into warm attire;
She loves as one who's seen the worst and knows
How gentle courage makes the whole world grow

Abuse Me No More

In shadow deep where silence dwells,
A heart once bound by whispered spells,
Through echoes past, the scars may show,
Yet I rise again, resolve to grow.
With chains unfastened, I reclaim my voice,
In the quiet strength, I make my choice.
No longer shall I bear the weight,
Of haunted nights and twisted fate.
The dawn break breaks forth, a promise clear,
A gentle whisper, "You need not fear."
With each step taken, the wind unwinds,
A tapestry of strength, where courage binds.
Abuse me no more, I declare with pride,
The wounds may linger, but hope is my guide.
With grace unyielding, I stand upright,
A beacon glowing through the long, dark night.
In every tear that fell like rain,
A testament of love, not loss or pain.
For in the tempest, I learned to soar,
Resilient spirit, I am so much more.
So let the of healing rise,
To scatter shadows, unveil the lies.
With heart unshackled and spirit free,
Abuse me no more; I am truly me.

Advance Citizens

In the land of wisdom and experience,
Where age is revered and,
Advanced citizens walk with grace and poise,
Their wisdom shines bright like a beacon.
With years of learning etched upon their faces,
They navigated the world with ease and precision,

Their mind are sharp and alert, always seeking,
New horizons to explore and conquer.
Their voices carry the weight of history,
Their words are a tapestry of lessons learned,
Guiding the youth with gentle patience,
Towards a future filled with promise and hope.
In their eyes, you see the depths of time,
A living reminder of the passage of years,
Yet in their heart, the fire still burns,
A passion for life that never wanes.
So let us honor these advanced citizens,
For they are the pillars of our society,
Guiding us forward with their wisdom,
enlightened tomorrow.

Alive With Purpose

In the dawn's soft light, we rise and shine,
With dreams ignited, hearts intertwine.
Each step we take, through valley wide,
Chasing the whispers of hope inside.
The mountains may loom, tall and steep,
But courage is sewn in the paths we keep.
With every challenge, a lesson unfolds,
In the tapestry of life, our story is told.
A dance with shadows, we fearlessly face,
Finding our rhythm, embracing each space.
With purpose as a compass, we chart the
unknown,
For every struggle, our strengths are grown.
The river of time flows, steady and true,
Reflecting the colors of dreams we pursue.
Together we weave a fabric so grand,
Where kindness and courage go hand in hand.
When the night draws its curtain, and
doubts arise,
Look to the stars, let your spirit fly high.
For every heartbeat rings out a song,
A melody of purpose, where we all belong.
So stand in the light, let your heart be bold,
For the world needs your fire, your story to

be told.
Alive with purpose, we journey together,
In the dance of existence, we'll shine forever.

Angry Woman

With fire in her eyes, she stands tall
A force to be reckoned with, she'll never fall
Burning with anger, fueled by rage
She's a tempest, ready to engage
Her voice was sharp like a sword,
Cutting through the air
No one dares to challenge her,
They best beware
For she's a warrior, fierce and strong
In her presence, all know they don't belong
Her passion ignites like a flame
Consuming everything, she has no shame
She will not be silenced, she will not yield
Her power and her fury, a mighty shield
So beware the wrath of this angry queen
For in her presence, all will glean
The strength and courage of a woman
scorned
In her fury, a legend is born.

Autistic Children Learns

In a world of constants and routines,
Autistic children find their means.
With minds that wanders and hearts that yearn,
They navigate a world to learn.
Through challenges and triumphs alike,
Each experience a chance to strike
A chord with their soul so deep,
Awaken talents they'll forever keep.
Their mind, a tapestry of vibrant hues,
Unraveling mysteries as they choose
To explore a world that may seem gray,
But to them, it's a vivid display.
They learn in ways unique to them,
Through patterns and rhythms, a priceless gem
Of knowledge and growth, each step they take,
A journey of discovery, a chance to make.
So let us walk beside them, hand in hand,
Supporting and guiding, helping them stand
As they navigate this world so unknown,
Autistic children, seeds of wisdom sown.

Awake

In the quiet of dawn, where dreams softly fade,
A whisper of hope begins to invade.
Deep within your soul, let the light ignite,
Kindle the fire in the stillness of the night.
Awake to the promise of each new day,
A chance to love, to grow, to find your way.
Let your heart be a compass, gentle and true,
Guiding you onward with skies of blue.
Every moment's a gift, a chance to believe,
In the strength of love, in the magic we weave.
Rise from the shadows, embrace your true face,
For in every breath, there's infinite grace.
Love is the sunshine that melts away fears,
A song in your heart that echoes through the years.
So awaken your spirit, let your dreams take flight,
Shine with fierce courage, in darkness and light.
In the depths of your being, know you are free,
Love is divine; love is eternity.
Awake to your purpose, let love be your guide,
And walk in the beauty of life, with arms open wide.

Awakening in the Here and Now

In the hush of dawn's embrace,
Let your spirit find its place.
Whispers of the morning light,
Guide your heart to take its flight.
Breathe in stories, nature waves,
In the rustling of the leaves.
Cultivate a garden sweet,
Where love and joy in blossoms meet.
Seek the smiles in every face,
Share your warmth, your love, your grace.
In the laughter, in the tears,
Find the hope that conquers fears.
Let compassion be your art,
With every beat, you mend a heart.
For peace is found in simple things,
In cherished moments, love takes wings.
So as you walk this wondrous Earth,
Embrace the joy, honor your worth.
In each heartbeat, in each breath,
Discover life beyond mere death.
Be present, and you'll surely see,
The beauty in just being free.
For in this life, our spirits soar,
Find peace, love, and happiness—explore!

Awakening the Inner Light

I step into the full version of myself,
Casting off shadows of doubt and fear,
Walking the sacred path within,
Where truth and silence intertwined.
Deep within a whisper stirs,
A divine voice unbound by time,
Revealing colors of my soul,
In hues beyond the earthly mind.
Breathe in the sacred air of now,
Feel the heartbeat of eternity,
Every pulse a reminder,
That I am part of infinity.
In this sacred awakening'
Self and universe dissolve as one,
And I emerge, luminous and free,
A spark of sacred eternity.

Awakening the Sacred Within

In the stillness where shadows fade,
A gentle whisper guides the way,
Unlocking the truths that softly cascade,
Lighting the dawn of a brand new day.
Feel the heartbeat of the universe,
Opening pathways to so much more.
Let your spirit soar beyond the sky,
Like a bird in a boundless stream,
Breathe in the hope, exhale the lie,
Awaken to your infinite dream.
Within your soul, a sacred flame,
Burn fiercely, bright and true,
A divine spark calling your name,
Renewing hope in all you do.
So rise, awaken, and be free,
Embrace the light, the love, the grace,
For in your heart's eternally,
Lies the sacred, timeless place.

Awakening Within

In the silent glow of dawn's first light,
A whisper stirs, a soul takes flight.
Beyond the mind's chaotic roar,
Lies a sacred, eternal core.
Breath like the wind, gentle and free,
Guides me to what I long to see—
The boundless space of inner grace,
A timeless, divine embrace.
With every heartbeat, I surrender more,
To love that's rooted in the core—
A sacred practice, pure and deep,
Awakening the soul from its sleep.
In stillness, I find the truth unfurled,
A divine spark in a restless world.
Deep awareness, a gentle wake,
A sacred journey I undertake.

Be True To Yourself

In a world of masks and facades,
Where pretense reigns, and falsehoods nod,
Be true to yourself, steadfast and bold,
Let authenticity be your stronghold.
Do not bend to the fickle ways,
Of those who seek to dim your blaze,
Stay true to the essence within,
Let your true self always win.
For in the sea of insincerity,
Your truth will shine like a rarity,
A beacon of light in the dark,
Guiding others to embark.
On a journey of self - discovery,
Embracing all of your complexity,
For when you live authentically,
You radiate a unique vitality.
So stand tall in your authenticity,
And revel in your individuality,
For when you are true to yourself,
You unlock boundless wealth.

Become More Beautiful

In the depths of your heart, a light resides,
A spark of the divine where love abides.
As dawn breaks gently, painting skies anew,
Know that my creation whispers back to you.
With every breath, let kindness flow,
Embrace the world with a heart aglow.
For beauty is not in a mirror's gleam,
But in the hearts touched by the dreams you dream.
Seek not perfection, for none are without flaws,
Embrace your journey, for therein lies the law.
In laughter and tears, in struggles that bind,
You'll find the strength that love has designed.
Let compassion guide every step you take,
In the shadows of sorrow, let hope awake.
For when you uplift those who feels small,
You become the most beautiful being of all.
So rise each day with a spirit so bright,
Our bond grows deeper when you share your light.
And as you reflect the Lord Almighty, in all that you do,
Remember dear one, that the Lord Thy God is proud of you.

Becoming the Light Within

Awaken soul, in silent grace you stand,
Beyond the shadows, in a boundless land.
Deep within, a whisper softly calls,
A sacred truth that quietly enthralls.
Unveil the mask, release the guise,
See the divine in your own eyes.
In every breath, in every beat,
The universe and you, in harmony, meet.
Feel the pulse of endless grace,
A gentle yearning to embrace your space.
You are the cosmos, vast and free,
Becoming who you truly are, eternally.
In sacred stillness, you unfold,
A story ancient, yet untold.
Deep awareness, pure and bright,
Guides you home through the endless night.

Believe and Achieve

In the depths of doubt, where shadows lay,
A spark ignites to lead the way.
With every heartbeat, with every breath,
You hold the power, defying death.
When storms may rage and mountain loom,
Your dreams are flowers that will bloom.
Trust in the strength that lies within,
Embrace the journey; let it begin.
For every step, though weary and long,
Creates a path where you belong.
With faith as your compass, courage your guide,
You'll sail through challenges with hope as your tide.
So rise, dear soul, let your spirit soar,
For you will make headway, and so much more.
Believe in yourself, let doubt fade away,
Your light will shine brighter with each passing day.

Beneath the veil of grace

In the shadows deep, where whispers twine,
A spirit stirs, resilient, divine.
You see a facade, so fragile, so meek,
Yet hidden within, a strength unique.
With every glance, you underestimate,
The fire that ignites, the will to create.
A tapestry woven with threads of resolve,
In silence I gather; in silence, evolve.
For very challenge that dares to confine,
I rise like a phoenix, through trials, I shine.
Your doubts, mere echoes, will fade into night,
As I navigate storms, emerge in the light.
The cloak of vulnerability, I wear with grace,
A guise, perhaps, but it's not my true face.
With wisdom as armor, and courage as my guide,
I stand undeterred, with strength and bona fide.
So, heed this truth, let perception expand,
The depths of my spirit, you'll barely comprehend.

For I'm not as helpless as you might assume,
In the garden of strength, I'll forever bloom.
With poise and determination, I carve my own path,

Through whispers and doubts, I summon my wrath.

So challenge your vision, and dare to redefine,
For the depths of my power, you will surely find.

49

Beneath the Weight of Struggle:

Beneath the weight of struggle, your spirit soared.
Breaking free from chains that once implored.
Every setback, a lesson; every loss, a gain,
Turning endless sorrow into an unyielding flame.
The echoes of doubt fade into different storms,
Replaced by the courage that now boldly forms.
A fortress built on perseverance and grace,
A testament to the power of the human race.
In the mirror, you see not just the scars,
But the shining light of a million stars.
For what was meant to shatter, to make you small,
Elevated you high beyond them all.
So march forward with unwavering might,
Hold fast to hope, ignite your light.
What tried to crush you—embrace the truth—
It only paved your way to eternal youth

Break the Chains, Become the Sky

Break the chains that bind your mind,
Leave the weight of doubt behind.
Light the lantern, feel the glow,
Step where healed horizons grow.
Whisper truths you used to hide,
Let your gentle courage rise.
Fear will fade — a passing sea,
You were never meant to flee.
Roots of old, they loosen slow,
New winds teach your courage to blow.
Gather hope like morning light,
Turn your wounds into wings in flight.
Breathe the dawn, unbar the door,
Walk toward the life you're for.
Mind unshackled, heart set free —
Rise, and reclaim your destiny.

Call Me Foxy Brown Sugar

Oh, call me Foxy Brown Sugar, the embodiment of elegance and
grace

My words drip like honey, my presence a dazzling embrace

In a world of chaos, I stand tall and strong
commanding attention with each and every song

I am the epitome of beauty and
power Combined

My soul radiates warmth, my spirit refined
With a flick of my mane, I capture all who see
Leaving them spellbound, yearning to be free
From the confines of their limitations, I inspire to rise

To reach for the stars, to soar through the skies
For I am Foxy Brown Sugar, a force to be reckon with

A beacon of hope, a light that will never dim
So when you hear my name, let it ring in your ears

A reminder that greatness is within, banish all fears

Call me Foxy Brown Sugar, the embodiment of all that is bold

For in my presence, the future unfolds.

53

Can't Keep a Good Woman Down

She's a force to be reckoned with,
A woman of strength and grace,
She's been knocked down before,
But she's never lost her faith.
She rises each time,
With fire in her eyes,

No matter what obstacles come her way,

She never fails to rise.
Her spirit is unbreakable,
Her courage knows no bounds,
She's a beacon of light in the darkness,
A true queen with a crown.
She's been through the fire and the storm
But she always comes out strong,
For you can't keep a good woman down,
Her resilience will never be gone.
So raise your glass to her,
For she's a force to be reckoned with,
A true inspiration to us all,
A woman who will always uplift.

Can't keep me down

Though trials may come and trouble may surround,

In my strength and perseverance, I am found.
No matter how hard they try to hold me back,
With my spirit and determination, I stay on track.
I rise above the obstacles in my way,
With unwavering resolve, come what may.
No force can hinder my progress or my will,
For I am unyielding, steadfast, and still.
Through darkness and doubt, I push forward With might

I am a force to be reckoned with, shining bright.
No one can break me, no one can keep me down,

For I am a warrior, wearing victory as my crown.
So try as they might to bring me to my knees,
I will rise up stronger, with the wind in my sails, unfree.

For I am unbeatable, unshakeable, and true,
No one can keep me down, for I will conquer, through and through.

Captivating Personality

She walks into the room with an air of grace,
A captivating presence that lights up the space.
Her smile is like the sunshine on a cloudy day,
Her laughter is contagious in every way.
With a twinkle in her eyes and a
confident stride,
She commands attention and cannot hide.
Her words are like music, soothing and sweet,
Her wisdom and charm are a true feat.
She captivates hearts with her elegant style,
A magnetic personality that leaves us beguiled.
Her aura is radiant, a beacon of light,
Guiding us through the darkness of night.
Oh, how are we drawn to her magnetic allure,
In her presence, we feel safe and secure.
A captivating personality, unique and rare,
With her around, we have nothing to fear.
So let us bask in her captivating glow,
For in her presence, we are content and know,
That a soul like hers is a precious treasure,
A gift to cherish and always treasure.

Captives

In chains we find ourselves bound,
Captives of fate's relentless grip
Trapped in shadows all around
In the depths of despair, we slip
But through our bodies may be confined
Our spirits soar, unchained and free
In the confines of the mind
We find the strength to break free
For even in the darkest night
A flicker of hope still burns bright
A beacon of courage, shining strong
Guiding us towards where we belong
So let us rise, rise up high
Cast off our shackles, touch the sky
For in our hearts, we hold the key
To unlock the door and set us free
No longer shackled, no longer bound
We'll break the chains that hold us down
And soar above, on wings of fate
No longer captives of our own hate.

Caught up in a whirlwind of emotions not mine

Being caught up in a whirlwind of emotions not my own is a disorienting and overwhelming experience. It often feels like being tossed around in a turbulent storm, with no clear path and no solid ground to stand on. It can leave me feeling confused, anxious, and powerless, as I struggle to make sense of the emotions that are swirling around me.

In these moments, it is essential to remember that the emotions I am experiencing are not my own, but belong to someone else. It is crucial to maintain a sense of perspective and detachment to avoid being consumed by intense emotions.

It is also important to practice self-care and set healthy boundaries to protect my emotional well-being. This may involve stepping back from the situation, seeking support from loved ones, or engaging in activities that help me relax and de-stress.

Ultimately, being caught up in a whirlwind of emotions not my own can be a challenging and draining experience. Still, by staying grounded, maintaining perspective, and taking care of myself, I can navigate these turbulent waters with grace and resilience.

Change Yourself For the Better

In the quiet dawn of a brand-new day,
Awaken your spirit, let fears drift away.
The mirror reflects not just what you see;
It holds the potential of who you can be.
Step boldly forward, embrace every chance,
For in the rhythm of life, there's a powerful dance.
With each beat of courage, let doubts turn to dust;
Transform your intentions, awaken your trust.
Like the butterfly breaking free from its shell,
Your journey to greatness begins with a swell.
Nurture your dreams, give your heart space to grow;
The seeds that you plant will flourish, I know.
Build bridges of kindness, extend a warm hand;
With every small effort, together we'll stand.
For change isn't daunting, it's a beautiful flight,
A path to a future where all can ignite.
So shed the old layers, let your true colors show,
The best version of you is waiting to glow.
Embrace every lesson, each stumble, each fall,
For change is a canvas, and you can paint it all.
Change yourself for the better, let your spirit ignite,
Shine bright in the world, be a beacon of light.
With love as your guide, and hope as your tether,
Together we'll flourish and change for the better.

Cherish Life

In the whisper of the morning breeze,
Lies the wisdom of the ages,
A call to rise with heartfelt ease,
As the world turns its pages.
Beneath the ever-watchful skies,
A tapestry of time unfolds,
In every dawn, a sweet surprise,
Life's secrets gently hold.
Each moment flows like rivers wide,
With lessons softly sung,
Embrace the silence, let it guide,
To know where we belong.
In nature's song and laughter's ring,
Find solace from the strife,
For in the heart of everything,
Lies the joy to cherish life.
Let gratitude bloom like a rose,
Its fragrance pure and bright,
Nurtured by love, as each day grows,
In a compassionate light.
Though shadows fall, as they will do,
And night descends its veil,
Remember, stars will see you through,
Where inner strength prevails.

So, cherish life with an open heart,
In every breath you take,
For even when the road departs,
A brighter dawn will wake.

Children

Tiny hands reaching for the sky,
Innocent eyes that sparkle and shine.
Children of wonder, full of delight,
Their laughter fills the air so bright.
Like delicate flowers in a field,
Their curiosity was never concealed.
Exploring the world with hearts so pure,
Their innocence is a treasure to endure.
With imagination wild and free,
They create worlds only they can see.
In their laughter, joy abounds,
Their innocence is a soothing sound.
Oh, the beauty of a child's mind,
So pure and gentle, so hard to find.
May we protect them, nurture and care,
For in their hearts, love is always there.
Let us cherish each moments with these little ones,

For they are the light that shines like the sun.
In their innocence, we find our way,
Guided by their laughter, each and every day.

Children Blessing Or Curse

In the eyes of children, a blessing divine,
Their laughter is pure, like sparkling wine.
In their innocence, a joy so immense
Their presence is a gift, a recompense.
But beware the curse that children may bring,
Their tantrums are fierce, like a storm in spring.
Their demands are endless, their patience thin,
Their energy is boundless, their mischief a sin.
Yet through it all, a parent's love prevails,
In their tiny hands, the future hails.
For in children, we see our reflection so clear,
Of our hopes, our dreams, even our greatest fears.
So cherish the blessing, endure the curse,
For raising children, we play nurse.
To their souls, their hearts, their minds So bright,

Guiding them towards the path of light.

Claim Your Light

You are not the shadow of another's praise –
You are the quiet dawn that keeps arriving.
Small as a seed, stubborn as a root, your worth
Presses up through ordinary dirt,
Remember: courage is often a soft decision, a
breathed "yes" after a night of doubts, a hand
Steadied on a seam of a new door, a voice
That learns to say the truth it owns.
Count your days by the kindness you give
Yourself, not by the trophies someone else
Displays. Your scars are maps, your mistakes
are lessons that teach your feet how to find the path again.

Stand with the steady, ordinary strength inside
You: a lighthouse built of patient mornings, a
sun that rises even through thin clouds – claim
your light, tend it, and let it be enough.

Clear The Cobwebs From Your Brain

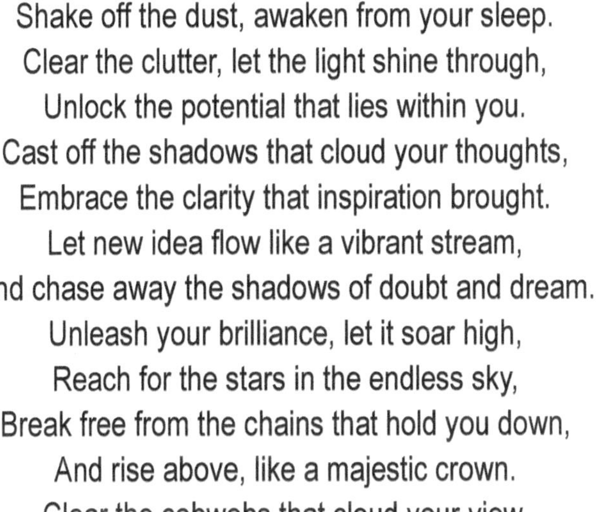

Oh wear mind, tangled in cobwebs deep,
Shake off the dust, awaken from your sleep.
Clear the clutter, let the light shine through,
Unlock the potential that lies within you.
Cast off the shadows that cloud your thoughts,
Embrace the clarity that inspiration brought.
Let new idea flow like a vibrant stream,
And chase away the shadows of doubt and dream.
Unleash your brilliance, let it soar high,
Reach for the stars in the endless sky,
Break free from the chains that hold you down,
And rise above, like a majestic crown.
Clear the cobwebs that cloud your view,
And embrace the world with a vision anew.
Let your mind wander, let your spirit fly,
And watch as your dreams reach the sky.
So clear the cobwebs from your brain,
And let your imagination reign.
For in the stillness of a clutter-free mind,
You'll find the inspiration you've been longing to find.

Crafted with Strength

I am who I am, by design, so divine,
God shaped my spirit, letting my light shine.
Resilient in heart, with wisdom I stand,
Blessed with a soul, crafted by His hand.
Through trials and storms, I rise, and I soar,
Each challenge faced opens a door.
With faith as my guide, I walk my true path,
Embracing my journey, all joy and all wrath.
I am a testament, strong and free,
A reflection of love, of grace, and of peace.
So here I proclaim, with a voice loud and clear,
I am who I am, and I hold my God near.

Cream Of The Crop

In the realm of excellence, where talent meet grace

Emerges the cream of the crop, the stars of the race

With skills honed to perfection, they stand proud and tall

Their brilliance shines brightly, outshining all
They are the chosen few, the top of their field
Their dedication unwavering, their
determination sealed
No obstacle too great, no challenge too tough
They conquer all with ease, their victory is enough

In their presence, we are humbled, in awe of their skill

Their passion and commitment are unbreakable will

They are the cream of the crop, the best of the best

Their success is a testament to their endless quest

So let us strive to follow in their noble path
To reach for greatness, to face the aftermath
For in the world of excellence, where dreams never stop
We seek to join the ranks of the cream of he crop.

Daring Boys

In a world where courage is rare,
Some daring boys do not scare.
They face the unknown with steadfast resolve,
Their hearts ablaze, their spirits involved.
With fearless passion burning bright,
They charge into the depths of night.
Brave and bold, they stand tall and true,
Fighting for justice, for all that is due.
Their bravery shines like a beacon of light,
Guiding the lost through the darkest night.
Challenging odds with unwavering grace,
They bravely confront every race.
Their strength and valor inspire us all,
Their daring deeds never do fall.
So heed the call of the daring boys,
For in their hearts, courage and joy.
May their fearless spirit never fade,
And in their footsteps, may we all wade.
For in a world so dark and cold,
The daring boys are worth more than gold.

Deep Knowing

Within the silence of my soul.
A truth so pure, so bold,
Resides beyond the mind's control.
A deep, eternal hold.
No need for words to confirm,
In stillness, I perceive—
A sacred knowing, long and firm,
A presence, I believe.
It whispers softly in the core,
A voice that's always near,
Unfolding wisdom, evermore—
The truth I hold so dear.
Deep in my heart, I understand,
A light that ever shines,
A guiding, gentle, sacred hand—
My deep, unending divine.

Do Not Fear What's Ahead

Do not fear what's ahead, for the unknown is but a canvas waiting to be painted with the brushstrokes of your courage. Embrace the uncertainty, for in it lies the potential for growth and transformation. Trust in the power of your spirit to guide you through the labyrinth of life, for you are more resilient than you know.

Let not fear be the chains that bind you, but rather the fuel that ignites your inner fire. Stand tall in the face of adversity, for challenges are but opportunities in disguise. Have faith in your journey, for destiny is a path that you alone must walk.

So lift your head high and march forward with unwavering conviction. The road may be long and winding, but with each step you take, you are one step closer to fulfilling your destiny. Do not fear what's ahead, for the future is yours to shape and mold. Embrace it with open arms, for you are destined for greatness.

Don't Give Up on Yourself

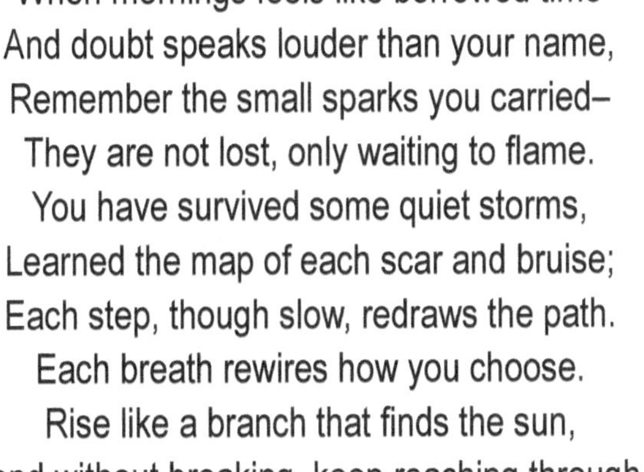

When mornings feels like borrowed time
And doubt speaks louder than your name,
Remember the small sparks you carried–
They are not lost, only waiting to flame.
You have survived some quiet storms,
Learned the map of each scar and bruise;
Each step, though slow, redraws the path.
Each breath rewires how you choose.
Rise like a branch that finds the sun,
bend without breaking, keep reaching through,
There is a pulse beneath the worry–
A steady yes that believes in you.
Turn the quiet into footsteps forward,
Trust the slow work of becoming whole.
Hold your heart like a stubborn seed:
You are the gardener, you are the soul.

Don't Let The Past Catch Up

In the shadows of yesterday, lies in the past forgotten and gray,

A weight that lingers, waiting to pull us astray,
But heed this warning, dear friend, do not let It binds,

For the future beckons, with hopes of a new kind.

Do not let the past catch up, with its chains of regret,

Let it fade into the distance, like a sun that has set,

Embrace the dawn of tomorrow with courage
and grace, and let the memories of yesterday find their rightful place.

For we are but travelers, on this journey
called life, and the past is but a chapter in a story of strife,

So let us forge ahead, with our heads held high,
And leave behind what once made us cry.
So do not let the past catch up, for it will only hold you back,

Embrace the unknown future, and stay on the right track,

For in the end, it is the choices we make,
That will determine the path we take.

Don't Underestimate Who I am

In the quiet corners of a restless mind,
Lies a spark, a fire, a strength defined,
Not by the whispers cold or doubting hands,
But by the resilience that is within me, I stand.
I am the dawn after a restless night,
A beacon shining, breaking through darkness
with light,

The melody in a storm's fierce roar,
A heart that's longing to soar even more.
Don't underestimate who I am,
For I carry worlds within my span,
A tapestry woven with hope and grace,
A fierce but gentle, unwavering face.
Beneath these scars, there's a story untold,
Of the battle fought, of losses bold,
And yet I rise, I stand, I breathe,
With newfound purpose, I seethe.
In every stumble, there's a lesson learned,
A restless spirit that's always burned,
Fueling dreams that refuse to die,
Reaching upward, aiming high.
So, judge not by what eyes perceive,
Nor by doubts that you believe,

For I am more than you can see,
A testament of tenacity.
Remember this when shadows creep,
And the world questions the promise I keep,
Don't underestimate who I am—
A story of hope, a rising lamb.

Eastern Star

In the eastern sky, a star shines bright,
Guiding us through the darkest night.
In the vast expanse of the universe,
It is a beacon of hope, a symbol of the diverse.

Its light whispers secrets of old,
Stories of love, of courage bold.
Ancient wisdom it holds within,
A reminder of where we begin.
Oh, eastern star, so pure and true,
With each flicker, a message anew.
Of peace and balance, harmony,
Of the interconnectedness we all see.
Luminous in the velvet night,
Dispelling shadows, casting light.
A celestial companion, a cosmic guide,
Into our hearts, forever to abide.
May we follow in your radiant path,
Embracing the beauty of the aftermath.
Oh, eastern star, forever we'll gaze,
In awe of your eternal blaze.

Echoes of the Balance

Karma is real—whatever you do will come back to you,

In ripples and returns, in shadow or in dew.
Plant kindness in the soil, and mercy will arise,
A harvest of soft light reflected in your eyes.
Harm another, build a wall with words or hands that bruise,

And time will roll its hourglass and teach the same old news.

The wheels spin not for judgment, but for lesson and for cure,

Each echo is a mirror asking, "Are you sure?"
Do good, you get good—like rivers finding seas
Do bad, you get bad—like storms that answer pleas.
Intent, a tinder spark; action, wind that fans the flame—

What you fling into the world returns to call your name.
Silent hearts remember debts no ledger could contain;

Grace repays the sleepless soul, remorse invokes its rain.

So walk with careful footsteps, speak with steady breath.

For every secret seed you sow will wake beyond your death.

Honor the small mercies, forgive the faults you see—

Balance is the altar where all spirits come to be.
Karma moves in subtle ways, in justice soft and true:

Whatever you do will come back to you, in one
form or another—do good, you get good; do bad, you get bad.

Embracing My Love

In this moment here, I stand tall and true,
No longer hiding from what I already knew.
Love whispers, calling my name,
A song of my soul, no longer a game.
I give myself the love I've long been denied,
A mirror of hope, shining with pride.
No more shadows, no more fears,
Just healing, courage, and wiping tears.
This present is mine, a gift divine,
In self-love's embrace, now I shine.
No more hiding, no more doubt,
Love's authentic voice is what I'm all about.
With every beat, my heart's renewed,
A love so deep, pure, and true.
In this moment, I found my way,
Loving myself, every day.

Emotions Running High

In the depths of my soul, emotions run high,
Like turbulent waves crashing against the sky.
A tempest of feelings, swirling within,
A storm of passion, ready to begin.
Love, like a wildfire, is consuming my heart,
Burning bright, tearing my world apart.
Joy, like a melody, lifting me high,
Soaring on wings, reaching for the sky.
Anger, like thunder, booming and loud,
Shaking my core, a dark, heavy cloud.
Sadness, like rain, pouring down fast,
Drenching my spirit, a storm that will last.
But in the chaos, there is clarity,
In the madness, there is sincerity.
Emotions running high, like a symphony,
Each note is a part of me, in perfect harmony.
So I embrace the storm, welcome the rain,
Ride the waves of emotion, embrace the pain.
For in the turmoil, I find my truth,
In the highs and lows, I find my youth.

Endurance: The Heart's Silent Triumph

In the quiet dawn of every soul's quest,
Lies a fire unquenched, a relentless zest.
Through storms and shadows, thick and deep,
Endurance whispers, "Rise, and keep the leap.
It is the steady pulse in trembling veins,
The whisper of hope amid the pains.
A mountain's weight, a river's flow,
Endurance bears what others throw.
Not born in ease, not forged in flight,
But in the struggle, born of night.
It molds the spirit, silent and strong,
Turning weakness into song.
With each stumble, a lesson learned,
In every scar, resilience burned.
The journey's long, the path unclear,
But hope remains forever near.
For endurance is the soul's true art,
A testament to a warrior's heart.
In every challenge, find your grace,
And triumph's smile will then embrace.

Everything is Going To Be Alright

When night presses close, and the city hushes low,
and every little doubt erects its shadowed signs,
remember: storms are teachers in a language bold,
and even the longest thunderline must end in light.
Breathe slowly. Name the fear like a small,
trembling bird perched at the window—
call it by the sound of rain.
You need not wake the whole world to prove your courage;
Courage often is the quiet hand that keeps the lamp.
Your wounds are cartographers of roads you've walked alone;
Their inked routes show where stubborn hope refused to break.
Each scar is not a verdict but a code for future maps:
How to steer through hidden swamps, how to trust dry ground.
There will be mornings when the mirror lies with tired eyes,
when your mouth forgets the cadence of its own proper name.
Still, there will be hands—perhaps rough, perhaps foreign—
reaching, and in that touch, some slight reprieve will learn
your shape.
Remember, the river does not hurry to arrive; it finds its way
around the cliffs, learning its own voice.
So can you: by patient making and by honest asking,
by loosening the rope of should, by tending one small task.
Hope is not a fragile bird that breaks if startled once.
It is a patient root that curves beneath the heaviest step,

finding cracks, sending shoots toward the impartial sun,
turning cold stone into a slow and green persistence.

(cont)
You are not only what faltered in the dark.
You are the ledger of little mercies you once kept:
a cup given, a promise kept, a laugh amid bad news—
all currencies that compound into light ahead.
When the world insists its verdict is a single loud word—
failure, loss, undone, let your softer ledger speak:
that the present is a room where the future can be built,
with planks of yesterday's lessons nailed to the window wide.
So lift your arms like sails.
Let small joys fill their seams: the plain coffee,
the letter you didn't know you'd,
the friend who calls and asks how the day was, really—
Plain questions that become the scaffolding of rescue.
Everything is going to be alright—
not as a sudden, blinding promise, but as a steady,
human work: patience, patching, choosing light.
It will be alright because you will find ways to keep going—
And because you are not alone in the art of learning to breathe.
Trust the slow revolution of gentleness within you.
Plant it, water it, speak kindly to its seedlings.
The future takes its shape from hands that keep on making.
Everything is going to be alright—one careful day at a time.

Evolution of the Soul

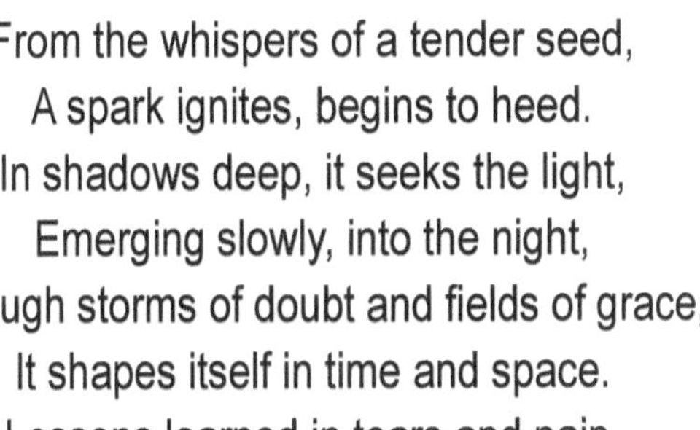

From the whispers of a tender seed,
A spark ignites, begins to heed.
In shadows deep, it seeks the light,
Emerging slowly, into the night,
Through storms of doubt and fields of grace,
It shapes itself in time and space.
Lessons learned in tears and pain,
Fostering strength from loss and gain.
Layers form like mineral veins,
Refining scars and breaking chains.
A journey woven, soul's design,
Transforming chaos into the divine.
No end in sight, just onward flow,
An endless dance, a steady grow.
The soul evolves, transcends, aspires—
An eternal flame that never tires.
It blooms anew in every breath,
A voyage born beyond death's depth.
From humble roots to stars above,
The souls' evolution, pure and love.
As dawn awakens every thought,
New horizons are softly sought.
Wisdom deependa, shadows fade,
A luminous path is softly laid.

In unity, it finds its kin,
Connecting hearts that dwell within.
Sharing light, dispelling gloom,
Building hope where fears loom.

The soul's ascent is gentle, sure,
A rise through clouds, a pure conure.
Each moment a new rebirth,
Unfolding truths of endless worth.
Boundless in its infinite quest,
Forever reaching, never rest.
Evolution's sacred dance,
A timeless, radiant advance.
In whispering soft, it learns to soar,
Unlocking doors to so much more.
The past dissolves into a stream,
Replaced by visions born of a dream.
Graced by love's eternal flame,
Each encounter fuels its name.
The essence pure, no longer bound,
In every loss, a gift is found.
It weaves through eternity's grace,
Expanding wisdom, embracing space.
From fragile beginnings to the whole,
The endless journey of the soul.
With every step, a deeper truth,
A silent voice, a sacred booth.
Forever growing, boundless, whole—
The everlasting evolution of the soul.

Fallout Shelter

In the depths of wasteland, underground
We hide
In our shelter, we reside, safe from the outside
Radiation above, monsters lurking in the dark
But we stay strong, united in our ark
Scavenging for supplies, searching for
hope
In this desolate world, we try to cope
With each passing day, we hold on to our faith
That someday we'll emerge into the light
we'll bathe
Through the trials and tribulations, we stand tall
Together we will conquer, we won't trip and fall
In this shelter we call home, we'll build a
new beginning
In this world of chaos, we'll find our
Own winning
So let the bomb fall, let the sky turn black
We'll stay strong; we have each other
And together we'll rise, as sisters and brothers.

Finding Peace Within

In the storm of life, where shadows loom,
And chaos dances in the silence of the room,
Remember this truth, let it settle like balm,
Peace is not the absence of trouble, but the
presence of inner calm.
Through valleys so dark and mountains so steep,

When worries surround you, and burdens seem deep,

Close your eyes, let the stillness come,
For peace is not the absence of trouble, but the presence of inner
calm.

When storms rage around you, and doubts start to creep,
Turn inward, where whispers of solace can leap.
In the depths of your spirit, let your heart become numb,

Knowing peace is not the absence of trouble,
but the presence of inner calm.
Seek not outside for a mirage of bliss,
For true serenity lies in moments like this.
With breath as your anchor, let your spirit succumb,

To the truth that peace isn't trouble's absence.

Embrace the chaos, let the waves crash and swell,

Find strength in your stillness, a sacred citadel.
Let love be the guidewhen the world feels less fun,
For peace is not the absence of trouble, but the presence of inner calm.
So when life overwhelms you, and you feel you're losing ground,

Remember, true tranquility in your heart can be found.

With hope in your soul, let go and then hum,
For peace is not the absence of trouble, but the presence of inner calm.

Forged in Thankfulness

I bow to the storm that shaped my hands —
the ragged rooms, the shouted nights,
the hands that bruised and tried to break me.
From chaos, I learned to name the wind,
to map each jagged scar as compass,
To build a hearth where none was offered.
Thank you to the ghosts of my beginning
who taught me endurance without meaning to,
whose absence taught me where to stand.
Thank you to the mirror of betrayal,
for teaching me the weight of my own voice,
how to carry it forward like a steady flame.
I keep the lessons, not the pain —
transforming every fracture into ladder rung.
I am both remedy and rebel, the slow, bright work of a steady hand.
From ruined rooms I planted gardens;
from trembling I became my own shelter.
To everyone who bent my arc —
the cruel, the careless, the lost, the kind —
I give my gratitude: clear and fierce.
You were the fire, the rain, the stone.
I am the house that stood when morning came,
and inside, I keep a light that will not go out.

Free Your Mind and Your Ass will follow

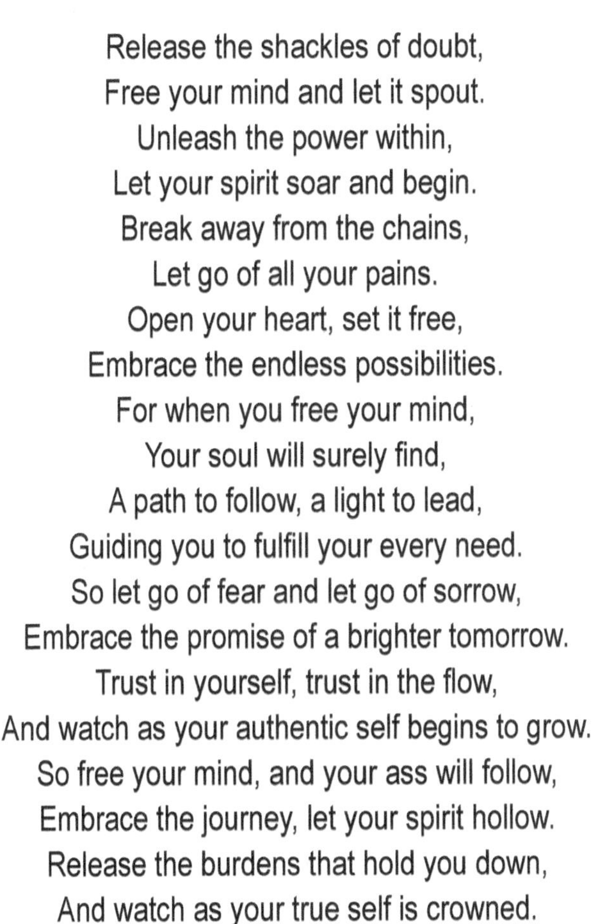

Release the shackles of doubt,
Free your mind and let it spout.
Unleash the power within,
Let your spirit soar and begin.
Break away from the chains,
Let go of all your pains.
Open your heart, set it free,
Embrace the endless possibilities.
For when you free your mind,
Your soul will surely find,
A path to follow, a light to lead,
Guiding you to fulfill your every need.
So let go of fear and let go of sorrow,
Embrace the promise of a brighter tomorrow.
Trust in yourself, trust in the flow,
And watch as your authentic self begins to grow.
So free your mind, and your ass will follow,
Embrace the journey, let your spirit hollow.
Release the burdens that hold you down,
And watch as your true self is crowned.

Free Yourself

Break the chains that bind you tight,
And rise to claim your right.
Free yourself from doubt and fear,
For your true purpose draws near.
Shake off the weight of past mistakes,
Embrace the power within you.
No longer trapped by others' expectations,
You are the captain of your own creations.
Let go of all that holds you back,
And step into the light without a lack.
Your potential knows no bounds,
As liberation in your heart resounds.
Fly like a bird with wings unfurled,
And let your spirit roam the world.
No longer shackled by conformity,
You are the author of your own destiny.
So stand tall and break free,
For in your soul, the key you see
Embrace the freedom that is your birthright,
And bask in the glow of your newfound light.

Freed by Grace, No Longer a Puppet

She once was bound by a silken string of doubt,
A puppet in the shadows, life's silent shout,
Controlled by whispers, chains of fear's design,
Lost in a maze where her true self is confined.
But then came the dawn, a whisper divine,
A voice of the heavens, a spark that did shine,
God's mercy unfolding, a healing embrace,
Breaking the chains that once held her in place.
No longer a pawn in another's game,
She steps into the sunlight, bearing her name,
A warrior of faith, with a heart set free,
Claiming her power, her destiny.
Her spirit now rises, unshackled and strong,
A song of renewal, a soul to belong,
In God's perfect plan, she found her part,
A masterpiece of courage, love, and heart.
From shadows to sunlight, she boldly proceeds,
A testament to grace, to hope, to her needs,
No longer a puppet, led by the hand,
She's dancing in freedom, in God's holy land.

From Shattered Dreams to Unbreakable Spirit

In the silent shadows where doubt took its stand,
A storm of challenges swept across the land.
Whispers of failure, a haunting refrain,
Yet within the silence, a fire remains.
What was meant to crush you, to bend and to break,
Turn into the ground where your roots did awake.
With every fall, you learn how to rise,
Transforming pain into strength and tears into skies.
Each scar a testament, a story of flight,
A beacon of hope in the darkest night.
The winds may have battered your fragile shell,
But strength was forged within that hell.
Now you stand taller, with a heart unbowed,
A symphony of resilience, proud and loud.
What was meant to crush you, in truth,
made you whole,
An unbreakable spirit, an unstoppable soul.

Futuristic Me

I dream of a soul that soars beyond the stars,
A heart that beats with hope, no matter how far.
In the mirror of time, I see endless grace,
A luminous future etched upon my face.
Through the shadows of doubt, I find my light,
A beacon of love in the eternal night.
Each step I take, with courage anew,
Builds the universe within me, true.
The future whispers in colors bright,
A symphony of dreams taking flight.
Futuristic me, alive and free,
A testament to what I am meant to be.
With love as my armor, faith as my guide,
I walk toward the dawn with pride.
For in the depths of the comic sea,
Lies the infinite potential of me.

Get Off Your Knees, Lift Your Head

Get off your knees, lift your head,
For greatness lies in you, unsaid.
Stand tall, against the tides of doubt,
With unwavering faith, push all boundaries out.
No longer bow to fear's cruel decree,
Rise up, tides of courage and strength to see.
You are a force, a beacon of light,
Shining bright, even in the darkest night.
Let your soul soar, like a bird in flight,
Embrace the power within, with all your might.
No more shall you cower or hide in shame,
For your worth surpasses all fame.
Get off your knees, embrace your worth,
For in your heart lies a treasure trove of earth.
Lift your head high, let your spirit shine,
For in your journey, a legacy divine.
So stand strong, against the winds of fate,
For you are destined for a greatness so great.
Get off your knees, lift your head,
And let your inner light be spread.

Get Rid of Negativity, Bring in the Positivity

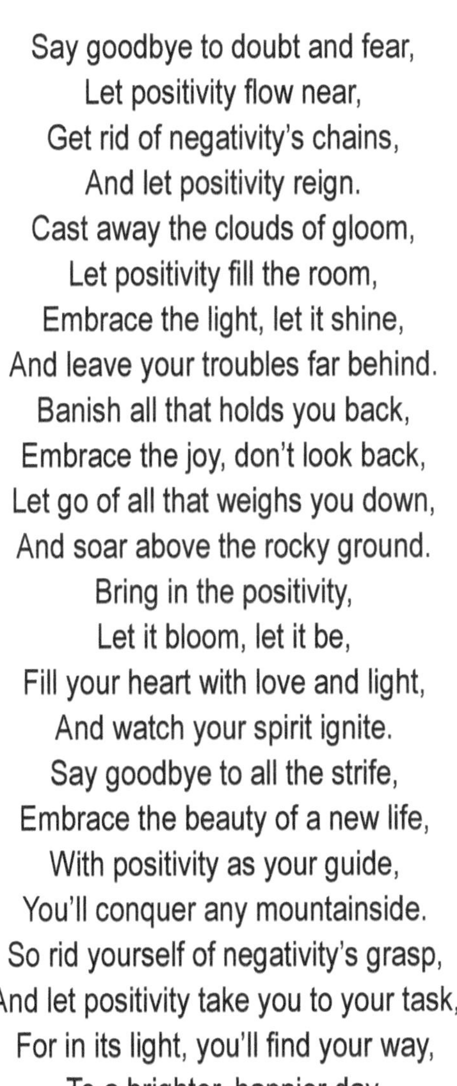

Say goodbye to doubt and fear,
Let positivity flow near,
Get rid of negativity's chains,
And let positivity reign.
Cast away the clouds of gloom,
Let positivity fill the room,
Embrace the light, let it shine,
And leave your troubles far behind.
Banish all that holds you back,
Embrace the joy, don't look back,
Let go of all that weighs you down,
And soar above the rocky ground.
Bring in the positivity,
Let it bloom, let it be,
Fill your heart with love and light,
And watch your spirit ignite.
Say goodbye to all the strife,
Embrace the beauty of a new life,
With positivity as your guide,
You'll conquer any mountainside.
So rid yourself of negativity's grasp,
And let positivity take you to your task,
For in its light, you'll find your way,
To a brighter, happier day.

Give Me a Moment

Give me a moment to catch my breath
As I navigate the twists and turns of life
Each step a silent battle against time
Give me a moment to feel the earth beneath My feet

To remind me of my place in this vast universe
Give me a moment to ponder the mysteries of existence

To marvel at the beauty of the world around me
And the fragility of human emotions
Give me a moment to cherish the fleeting moments of joy

To hold onto the memories that sustain me in the darkest times

Give me a moment to reflect on the choices I have made

To learn from my mistakes and strive for a better tomorrow

Give me a moment to appreciate the simple pleasures

That brings color to the dull canvas of everyday life

Give me a moment to breathe in the fresh air of possibility

To embrace the unknown with an open heart
And the courage to face whatever lies ahead
Give me a moment to be grateful for all that I have

And the strength to carry on when all seems lost

Global Village

In a world stitched by thread unseen,
Cultures collide, where dreams convene.
Voices rise in a harmonic flight,
A tapestry woven in day and night.
From ancient sands to mountain peaks,
In every tongue, a story speaks.
The rhythm of laughter, the pulse of the street,
In this global village, our hearts find beat.
Bridges of hope, where borders dissolve,
In unity's embrace, our puzzles resolve.
With hands intertwined, diversity thrives,
A mosaic of colors, where humanity strives.
Echoes of wisdom, from ages long past,
In shared aspirations, our legacies are cast.
Through trials we wander, in joy we intertwine,
In the garden of life, together we shine.
With every shine rise, a canvas reborn,
We paint a new future, with love, not scorn.
Let dialogue flourish, let kindness prevail,
In this global village, our spirits set sail.
So cherish the moments, the bonds we create,
In the heart of this village, we celebrate fate.
For together we journey, through shadows
and light,
As one, we are stronger, united in flight.

Guided by the Eternal Light

I shall not fear the shadow's play,
Or in the dawn, I find my way.
Beyond the veil, where spirits soar,
A radiant love forevermore.
The light within my soul will shine,
A sacred bond, divine, divine.
Death's gentle whisper, a new beginning,
An endless journey, peace descending.
Embrace the sky, the endless height
Where darkness fades in sacred light.
I go with faith, my heart held tight,
Guided by love into the night.

Head Held High

With head held high, I face the world,
In strength and grace, my flag unfurled.
No storm can shake my firm resolve,
No challenge daunts, my fears dissolve.
I walk with purpose, unafraid,
My path is clear, my plan well-laid.
With every step, I rise above,
A shining beacon of hope and love.
For I am strong, in heart and mind,
A steadfast spirit, pure and kind.
No doubt can cloud my steady gaze,
No fear can dim my steady blaze.
So let the world try its best,
To bring me down, put me to the test.
I'll stand tall, with head held high,
And face each trial with a resolute eye.
For I am the master of my fate,
With head held high, I conquer hate.
I am the captain of my soul,
With head held high, I reach my goal.

Higher Heart

I wake to the morning, gentle by grace,
A mirror of courage in a steady, warm place.
I honor my truth, let honesty sing,
Roots in compassion, like birds on the wing.
I tend to my wounds with forgiveness and care,
Feed seeds of gratitude, spouting light from despair.
I give from abundance, not fear or regret,
Knowing my worth is more than the debts I forget.
Each breath is a pledge to the values I hold —
Brave, kind, and faithful, my spirit grows bold.
I walk toward purpose, my steps soft and sure,
Self-love as my compass, my path clear and pure.
I listen for wisdom in silence and songs,
Trusting the cadence that guides me along.
With patience I flourish, with mercy I rise,
Seeing my edges as stars in my skies.
I honor the journey, each stumble and climb,
Knowing growth keeps its rhythm in time.
I stand in connection with truth, with the whole —

A lighthouse of purpose, a steady, kind soul.
So I offer myself grace and cultivate peace,
Let pride in my progress and wonder increase.
Rooted in values that bless and set free,

I am love, I am ready, exactly where

I'm meant to be.

I Am a Phenomenal Black Woman:
Walk With Dignity, Move With Power

In the mirror, I see the reflection, real and true,
A queen with a crown of resilience, breaking through.
Walk with dignity, head held high, spirit soaring free,
A testament to strength, unbreakable, and key.
My roots run deep in history's sacred soil,
Every challenge faced turns into divine toil.
Move with power, fire burning fierce and bright,
Illuminating paths through the darkest night.
I am the voice of ancestors, proud and strong,
Singing songs of hope, righting every wrong.
In every step, I embrace my worth and grace,
A phenomenal Black woman, destined to shine in this space.

Let my journey inspire, let my story be told,
A legacy of courage, fierce and bold.
With dignity and power, I rise, and I stand,
A force of love, a miracle planned.

I Am Capable of Deep Self-Healing and Uninterrupted Optimistic Conversion

In the depths of my heart, where shadows once lay,
I uncover the light that grows stronger each day.
With whispers of hope and the strength of my will,
I rise from the ashes, empowered and still.
Through valleys of struggle, past mountains of doubt,
I venture with courage, releasing my shout.
Each tear that I shed, a river of grace,
Paves the way for healing and reclaiming my space.
Embracing the lessons, the scars, and the pain,
I scatter the darkness, breaking every chain.
For within me there dwells a resilient spark,
Igniting my journey, dispelling the dark.
With each breath I take, I gather my might,
Transforming my shadows into purest light.
A dance of unfolding, each moment a gift,
In the art of self-healing, my spirit will lift.
I am the artist, and life is my canvas,
With colors of courage, my dreams I'll enhance.
Through rainbows of visions, I find my true way,
In the embrace of my power, I'll flourish and sway.
The whispers of doubt may at times intertwine,
Yet I hold the belief that my journey is mine.

With roots deep in wisdom and branches that soar,
I cultivate growth, my spirit will roar.
So here I stand tall, a beacon of change,
Willing to grow, allowing the strange.
For each step I take, I'm affirming my claim,
I'm capable of healing, igniting my flame.
Transforming my life with each thought I align,
Embracing the beauty of my own design.
Thus, I walk forward with passion and zeal,
For I am a healer, my heart is a wheel.

I Am Stronger Than You Think

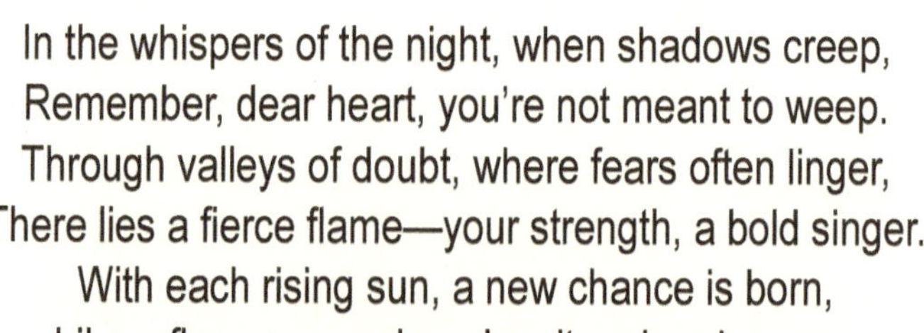

In the whispers of the night, when shadows creep,
Remember, dear heart, you're not meant to weep.
Through valleys of doubt, where fears often linger,
There lies a fierce flame—your strength, a bold singer.
With each rising sun, a new chance is born,
Like a flower emerging, despite a harsh scorn.
When storms shake your world, and
darkness surrounds,
Stand tall, for within you, true courage abounds.
Like mountains that crumble, yet stand through the years,
You've faced many battles, and you conquered your fears.
Each scar tells a story, each tear marks a fight,
A testament of power, glowing ever so bright.
So gather your dreams, let them soar through the skies,
Embrace every challenge, let hope be your rise.
For you are a warrior, a spirit unchained,
With love in your heart, and strength uncontained.
When whispers of "can't" fill the air like a fog,
Remember the fire, you're capable, strong.
With each step you take, let your spirit unfold—
You are stronger than you think, a story retold.
In the tapestry woven, in colors so bold,
Your journey's alive, a magic to behold.
So rise, dear heart, let your light brightly link,
For you are a wonder—far stronger than you think.

I Cultivate My Growth, My Spirit Will Roar

In the garden of life, where the wildflowers bloom,
I nurture each seed, for they chase away gloom.
With the sun as my guide and the rain as my friend,
I cultivate my growth, and on this path, I ascend.
Each challenge I face is a stone in my way,
But I'll dig deeper still, through the heat of the day.
For the strength is not found in the moments of ease,
But in the trails that shape me, like roots in the breeze.
I learn from the shadows that dance on the ground,
In silence, I gather wisdom profound.
With petals of courage, I blossom and thrive,
In the rich soil of hope, I feel so alive.
My spirit will roar like a lion set free,
Awakening dreams that were hidden in me.
With fire in my heart and a vision so clear,
I embrace every moment, I shed every fear.
For life is a journey, a beautiful quest,
With each step I take, I am truly blessed.
I cultivate my growth, as the sunsets ignite,
A symphony of colors, my soul takes flight.
So here in this moment, I rise, and I soar,
With every new dawn, I'll embrace and explore.
The world is a canvas, and I am the art,
I cultivate my growth with love in my heart.

I Thought I Would Survive

I thought I would survive my childhood—
patchwork summer stitched with whispered prayers,
soft promises tucked into hollowed pillows,
the small bravery of keeping dawn at bay.
I thought I would find my Prince Charming,
someone with hands that knew how to hold light,

a voice that mended the cracked place in me,
a map to lead lost footprints home.
Instead, I found the son of Satan—
A smile that learned to worship ruin,
fingers that catalogued my fractures like trophies,

a laugh that turned the tender into contraband.
He taught me how to misname love as terror,
how to swallow quietly until it becomes a stone,
How nights can teach me a body to forget morning.
I planted gardens in the ghost of him.
They spouted weeds that spoke in his breath.
I learned the language of footsteps that never left,
The grammar of apologies meant nothing at all.

Yet beneath the ash, a stubborn
root remembers—

the child who skinned her knee
and kept walking,

the small pulse that once believed in sunrise,
the art of gathering broken things and calling them mine.

I thought I would survive my childhood—
I thought I would find a hand that fit mine.
I was wrong about the Prince, but not about surviving:
each day, I pry a little light from the dark,
and learn how to call my own name again.

I Will Not Lie Down And Die

In the face of adversity, I declare with resolve
I will not lie down and die; I will rise and evolve
For I am stronger than the challenges that arise
I will face them head-on, with unwavering eyes
Though darkness may surround me, I will not falter

I will push through the storm, refusing to alter
My determination, my courage, my drive
I will not be defeated, I will thrive
I will not succumb to the fears that loom
I will stand tall, unyielding, in the face of oom
For I am a warrior, with a fire in my soul
I will not lie down and die; I will reach my goal
So let the obstacles come, let the
darkness descend
I will not be broken, I will not bend
I will rise above, I will conquer and soar
For I am a fighter, forever more.

Inquiries of the Mind

Oh, are you daft, my earnest soul,
To wander 'neath the shimmering moon?
In the shadows deep where whispers toll,
Do thoughts of twilight's dance attune?

Your gaze, it falters, vision blurred,
In realms where reason bends and sways,
Do fleeting dreams, like songs unheard,
Not beckon forth through starry ways?

Let not the chaos dwell within,
For clarity shall lead your stride.
In labyrinths where doubts begin,
With a steadfast heart, let calm abide.

Shall folly reign o'er gentle thought?
Or wisdom weaves the threads of fate?
In every choice, let truth be sought;
Resilience stands where fears await.
so when the tempest darkly calls,
And reason seems a distant shore,
Remember now as silence falls,
Your spirit strength shall ever soar.

Oh, are you daft, my thoughtful friend?
In reverie, let clarity blend.
For in the quest, through trails vast,
The dawn shall break; the night won't last.

It's Time To Leave The Negative Behind

It's time to bid farewell to the darkness within,

Shedding burdens and releasing the sin.
No longer shall we dwell in despair,
For there is hope and light to repair.
Let go of the toxic thought that weighs you down,

Embrace the beauty that surrounds.
Release the grip of doubt and fear,
And watch as positivity draws near.
Rise above the storm clouds that loom,
And dare to chase after brighter days in bloom.

Leave behind the shadows of the past,
And embark on a journey that will forever last.

Negativity only hinders our growth,
But with optimism, we find our worth.
So let us break free from the chains that bind,

And march forward with a clear mind.
It's time to leave the negative behind,
And embrace the positivity that we find.
Let us journey toward the brighter tomorrow,

Where joy and peace erase our sorrow.

It's Time You Start Choosing You

You've been the lighthouse bending toward their shore,

A candle burning low to give them more.
You stitch the seams of other people's nights,
And swallowed storms to ease their smallest frights.

You learned to speak in quiet, soft tones,
To trade your edges for their brittle thrones.
You memorized the maps that led you home,
While wandering your own streets, afraid to Roam.

But there's a voice inside that's patient, true—
A gentle knuckle tapping: choose you.
Not careless, not a shout that breaks the sky,
But steady, like the tide that will comply.
Choose the mornings when your coffee tastes like light,

Choose the nights that don't demand you dim your sight.

Choose friends who honour what you try to be,
And lovers who reflect, not steal, your sea.
Choose boundaries that bloom like honest springs,
Choose time to grieve, to grow, to learn new things.
Choose all the pieces you have tucked away—

The parts you told yourself would wait someday.
If fear still stands at your familiar door,
Remember, courage is a thousand smalls, not war.

One yes, one no, one breath that's purely yours,

A quiet turning toward untethered shores.
So rise, not for the world to watch or prove,
But for the tender heart that needs your move.
It's not neglect to tend your own bright view—
It's sacred work: at last, begin choosing you.

Karma

Do not let the past become your life's chain creed:

It's only meant to be the lesson, not the law.
Each scar is a turning point, each loss a seed
that breaks in faithful earth to teach you more.
When shadows rise and whisper old regrets,

Reply with steady breath and softer eyes.
The soul's account counts lessons, never debts;

For growth repays what memory supplies.
Forgive the echoes that would steal your dawn,

they're mirrors, not the captors of your fate.
Walk gently through the ruins you've outgrown;
They are the thresholds that make wisdom wake.
Pain is a teacher wearing humble clothes,
and compassion is the coin you spend to heal.

Release the past — let healing rivers flow;
True freedom is the choice to stand and feel.
Karma keeps no ledger of your shame,
It turns each fallen stone into fertile ground.

Become the light that answers to no blame;
in the present breath, your sacred peace is found.

Knock Me Down: I'll Pick Me Up

In the quiet shadows of despair's embrace,
Where shadows linger and fears find their place,
You knocked me down with relentless force,
But within my heart, I chart my course.

For every fall, a chance to rise,
In brokenness, my spirit flies,
A phoenix born from ashes deep,
Awakening strength from veins that weep.

Your blows may shake my fragile ground,
Yet in my core, a voice is found—
A whisper fierce, a battle cry,
That I am deep, unbreakable, and high.

The journey's long, the road is steep,
But hope ignites, and dreams run deep,
Each scar a story, a lesson learned,
From every wound, a fire burned.

No storm too fierce, no night too long,
My courage sings a hopeful song,
I stand again, resilient and free,
Embracing all that's meant to be.

So let the world keep knocking away,
I'll rise anew with each new day—
For in my soul, I always know,
The strength to grow, the will to glow.

When you knock me down, I'll be there to pick me up,
A resilient heart, endless and tough,
Walking forward, unafraid, unbroken,
A promise kept, a spirit awoken.

Living My Truth

In the sunlight's warm embrace,
I find my rhythm, my own pace.
With every step and every cheer,
I shine my light, dispelling fear.
Authentic self, a vibrant song,
In my own skin, where I belong.
Heart wide open, I dance and sway,
Living my truth, come what may.
So here's to freedom, bright and bold,
A story of courage, waiting to be told.
With love as my guide, I lift my voice,
In this beautiful life, I rejoice!

Men, Treat Your Woman Like a Queen

In a world where love's not always seen,
Men, treat your woman as a precious queen.
With tender grace and steady hands,
Cherish her heart, fulfill her demands.

When she rises bright, a beacon of light,
Honor her dreams: keep them in sight.
With kindness and laughter, through joy and pain,
Together you'll dance in the softest rain.
She's your partner, your balance, your shining star,
In the journey of life, she's never too far.

Give her respect, let your love's voice sing,
As she treats you nobly, like the king you bring.
In the moments of doubt, be her sheltering tree,
Let understanding flow, set her spirit free.

With patience like rivers and love that won't wane,
You'll both build a kingdom, not one built in vain.
So hold her hand, through the highs and lows,
In the garden of love, let your trust be the rose.

For when you uplift her, the bond will take wing,
Men, treat your woman as a queen; never sting.

In return, she'll honor your castle's grand halls,
With loyalty woven through love's gentle calls.

together, you'll thrive, in passion's sweet ring,
Men, treat your woman as a queen; you're her king.
Let your hearts be the chorus, let your spirits entwine,
In the dance of true love, both yours and mine.

For when kindness flows freely, and respect is the thing,
A man treats his woman as a queen, a true king.

Mind Your Business

In the realm of daily affairs,
It's wise to heed this solemn prayer,
"Mind your business with great care,
And leave others' burden to bear."

For in this bustling world we dwell,
Gossip spreads like wildfire's swell.
But true success does not reside,
In prying eyes and tongues that chide.

So focus on your own pursuits,
And let your actions speak for you.
For those who meddle in affairs,
Will find a tangled web ensnares.

Keep your gaze on what's in sight,
And let others live their plight.
So heed this warning, clear and bold,
And watch your own dreams unfold.
Mind your business, stay on course,

And let success be your driving force.

Move Forward Don't Look Back

Onward we stride, toward the light,
Letting go of the past defeats in our sight.
Forward we move, with courage and grace,
Leaving behind what we can't embrace.
Don't look back, for the future awaits,
With endless possibilities and open gates.
Embrace the journey, with faith and trust,
In the unknown lies our true and just.
Each step we take, with purpose and might,
Guided by hope, shining so bright.
no longer bound by what once held us down,
We rise above, wearing victory as our crown.
Let go of doubt, let go of fear,
For in this moment, we find our share.
Strength and resilience, within our core,
Moving forward, seeking more and more.
Don't look back, for we are meant to soar,
To reach new heights never seen before.
With every breath, with every step,
We move toward our destiny, no regrets.

My Hands Are Bound

In twilight's grasp, my hands are bound,
By shadows deep, where dreams confound.
Each whispered a tale, a silent plea,
Entrapped in fate, I yearn to be free.

The chains of doubt, like serpents, cling,
While echoes of resolve softly spring.
In moments lost, where courage wanes,
A flicker glows through hidden pains.

Oh, let the winds of change arise,
To lift the veil from weary eyes.
With a fervent heart, I seek the light,
To break these bounds and take to flight.

In solemn grace, I find my strength,
Through trials faced, I'll go the length
Though shadows loom and silence reigns,
Resilience stirs within my veins.

So hear my call, oh stars above,
Guide my hands, ignite the love.
For though I stand with barrier wide,
My spirit's fire cannot be denied.

In every tether, a story is penned,
A journey vast, where sorrow mend.
With purpose clear, I shall rise,
For even bound, the soul can climb the skies

Ode To Self-Discovery

In a quiet chamber of the heart, I dwell,
Where whispers of the soul begin to swell.
With every tear that graced my
trembling cheek

I found the strength in shadows, soft yet meek.
Through the mirrored path of doubt and fear I roamed,
With shattered fragments of a heart uncombed.
But in the silence, truth began to shine,

A sacred journey, woven thread divine.
To loveself– a craft both bold and rare,
A tapestry of wounds, now laid bare.
In valleys deep, where echoes gently fade,

I forged a bond with myself, alone, unafraid.
Boundary walls, once held in scorn, have Crumbled low,
Revealing roots of love, where blossoms grow.
A symphony of strength in every breath,

Embracing life, defying quiet death.
In every flaw, a masterpiece I find,
The rise of spirit, unfettered and unkind.
With open arms, the world comes into view,

For loving oneself births love anew.
So here I stand, with courage as my crest,
In learning to love myself, I have been blessed.
With vibrant grace, I walk this tender road,

A sovereign heart, where seeds of
kindness flowed

Old Oak Tree

Oh, ancient oak, with branches wide
and strong
Your leaves whisper secrets of days
long gone
Majestic and wise, your roots run deep
A silent sentinel, your watch to keep

Through wind and storm, you stand tall
A testament to resilience through it all
Your crooked limbs tell tales untold
Of history and memories, forever enfold

Oh, oak tree, with bark so rough
Each line and crevice tells of rebirth
Seasons come and seasons go
But you remain steadfast, in ebb
and flow

In your shade, creature finds solace
From blazing sun and life's malice
A sanctuary of peace and calm
Beneath your boughs, a soothing balm

Oh, ancient oak, with wisdom untold
In your presence, time unfolds
A living legend, from days of yore
Forever standing, strong and sure.

Once In A Lifetime

In the fleeting moments of our lives,
There comes a chance, a rare surprise.
A once-in-a-lifetime gift so grand,
That led us to new paths, to new lands.

Embrace the moment, seize the day,
For time is swift, it does not delay.
Opportunities like this are few,
So cherish them, let them renew.

A pure love, a dream so bright,
A once-in-a-lifetime, a beacon of light.
Hold it close, treasure it well,
For in its presence, all will swell.

Do not let fear or doubt take hold,
For in this moment, you are bold.
Embrace the challenge, face the test,
And you will rise above the rest.

Once in a lifetime, it's now or never,
So grasp it tight, and hold it forever.
Let it guide you, let it inspire,
And set your soul on fire.

Our Work Has Just Begun

As the sun rises in the east,
Our work has just begun,
With courage in our hearts,
And determination in our souls.

With every task we undertake,
With every challenge we face,
We stand strong and united,
As we strive for excellence.

The road ahead may be long,
The journey may be tough,
But we are not afraid,
For we are warriors at heart.

With passion in our eyes,
And a vision in our minds,
We press forward with purpose,
And a relentless dive to succeed.

So let us forge ahead,
And conquer every trial,
For our work, has just begun
And together, we shall prevail.

Quiet Fortitude

When words arrive like storm-wet stones to throw,
And pride breaks glass in rooms where echoes stay,
I learn a different harvest — soft and slow —
To plant my silence where my tempers fray.

The urge to answer sharply with equal heat
is loud and tempting, pulsing in my chest;
But calmer breath and measured, steady feet
Turn anger's fire to something kinder, blessed.

Respect once met each time with roaring guard
Will harden hearts and build brittle walls.
So I untangle fury, keep the yard
Where patience sweeps, and teaches me to fall

into a steadier center, where I see
That dignity need not demand return.
A quieter armor shields a more gentle me,
And help a humbled, wiser self to burn.

I count the seconds like a string of beads,
Each one is a bead that cools the sting of shame.
I answer later, not because it feeds
Their triumph, but because I chose my name.

For calm is not surrender, not defeat —
It's choosing soil where better roots will grow;
It's quiet hands that turn the other cheek,
Not because I'm weak, but because I know.

That every clash can teach a softer art:
How boundaries bend, how silence can be stern.
The strength that holds its tongue is not apart
from courage; it's the courage to unlearn

The scripts that scream for fists or biting words,
To let a wiser cadence claim the day.
A steady voice, like birds among the firs,
Reminds me how to love myself and stay.

So if you wound me with contempt or slight,
I will not mirror thunder with my roar.
I'll light a lantern in the folding night,
and watch my inner garden grow once more.

This different kind of growth is slow, profound —
A calm that keeps its honor and its truth.
In gentleness, my truest self is found,
And in restraint I find the bloom of youth.

When storms recede, my patience stand revealed:
Not hollow peace, but power underneath.
Respect returns when hearts are gently healed,
Or else I walk on steady, sure of breath.

The world will shout; I'll answer in my time,
With words that carry salt and steady flame
To stay calm when disrespected is sublime —
A quiet victory with no one to blame.

135

Ready to Face the World

I)
I wake with sunlight stitched to the window,
a thin, steady thread of gold that
sews the night's loose edges into morning.
There is a quiet courage in the small Things

a kettle hiss, a breath that expands like lungs
learning to hold the ocean.
I tie my shoelaces with careful fingers —
knots that memorize the promise of movement

and step into the day as one steps into a new language:
clumsy at first, then clearer with the syllables.
I have known fear as a room that closes,
its air thick with "what if" and the hum of
doubt.
But fear is only a bell: it rings, and I answer
, not by fleeing, but by letting sound t
each me where the walls are weak.
I press my palm to those places and

find they give, a little at a time, until a doorway opens.
Beyond it: noise, color, the risk of falling,
and the steadiness of the ground
when you keep walking.

II)
There are days when the world looks like a ledger:
columns of losses and gains tallied in a precise, cold hand
. I remember names I can't return, promises
that frayed, and the heavy gold of regret.

Yet even ledgers cannot contain every miracle.
The margin is wide with possibility;
I draw there with a sharpened hope.
I write in capitals the small victories:

a phone call that mended a distance, a meal
shared with laughter that did not need sweetness,
a glance exchanged with a stranger that felt like home.
I carry scars like constellations under my skin,

Maps of where I leaned too hard on living.
They glitter slightly when the light hits —
proof that repair leaves stars.
The world offers weather: storms that tear flags down,

winters that close doors,
afternoons that bruise the face of patience.
But weather passes; the soil remembers how to hold seed.
I learn to be a careful gardener of my day,
watering what is honest, pruning what pretends.

III)
To face the world is not a single battle
cry but the patient cadence of showing
up again.
It is the art of forgiving the mirror for yesterday's failing, and teaching
your shadow to keep pace with your steps.

It is asking for help when your hands are full,
and offering help when your hands are full,
and offering help when others' hands tremble too.

We are not islands drafting our own tides.
We are an archipelago of reaching arms,
bridges built by kindness and the slow,
steady work of trust.

Restore Order

In the quiet whisper of dawn's soft light,
A silent call awakens the soul's deep night.
Shattered pieces, scattered wide,
Yearn for the touch of the divine guide.
Breathe in hope, exhale the fear,
Let wisdom's voice become so clear.
From chaos blooms the gentle plan,
A sacred dance within every man.
Flow like rivers, steady and strong,
Finding rhythm where hearts belong.
Restore the balance, mend the broken,
Hear the unspoken, the silent token.
In stillness, find your sacred ground,
Where peace and love are truly found.
The universe hums in sacred accord—
A divine symphony, restored by the lord.
Within the silence, spirit's flame,
Ignite the path, renew the name.
No more turmoil, no more strife,
Just a gentle, sacred life.
Trust in the universe's tender art,
Healing begins within the heart.
Every breath, a sacred prayer,
Bringing order from despair.

Rise from shadows, embrace the light,
Transform the darkness into bright.
With each step, a new start—
Restore order, heal the heart.
In divine harmony, find your way,
A timeless dance, night and day.
Let love's pure song resound—
In harmony, we are bound.

Return

Long have I wandered, far from home,
Yearning for the day when I return.
Through trials and tribulations I did roam,
Yet my heart did always burn.
To see the familiar sights once more,
To feel the embrace of loved ones near,
To know that I am not alone,
That my journey was not in vain, I cheer.
The road was rough, the way was steep,
But the promise of a homecoming kept Me whole.

And now, as I finally reach the keep,
I am filled with joy, with pride, with soul.
For I have returned, triumphant and strong,
To the place where I belong,
And though the journey was long,
I know now that I am where I truly thrive, where
I truly thrive.

Rise to the Light

Lift your spirit, soar above,
Where gentle breezes sing of love.
Tune your mind to comic rhyme,
Embrace the glow of higher time.
Let kindness flow like endless streams,
Awaken dreams within your beams.
Ascend beyond your earthly chain,
Where peace and joy shall never wane.
Feel the pulse of sacred grace,
Embed serenity in your space.
Vibrate with truth, with hope, anew,
A luminous soul shining through.
In higher vibration, find your glow,
A radiant light you're meant to show.
Elevate your heart's pure song,
And in love's harmony, belong.
Let fear dissolve as shadows fade,
In sacred glow, let doubts evade.
With every step and breath you take,
Awaken more for kindness' sake.
Connect with stars that softly gleam,
Awaken your most radiant dream.
The universe responds with a
gentle sway,

Aligning your heart along love's way.
So raise your vibrations high and free,
Embrace the boundless energy.
In higher realms, your spirit thrives,
A beacon of eternal drives.
Feel the whisper of the divine,
A sacred song in every line.
Let gratitude be your guide,
With open arms, stride with pride.

Harmony flows in every breath,
Transcending all that binds or rests.
Align with love, pure and vast,
Unlock the magic, make it last.
In this radiant, elevated space,
Find your truth, your sacred place.
So walk in light, let worries cease,
And live within eternal peace.

Rising from Shadows

Watch me as I crumble your lies beneath my feet,
With every step I take, your deceit finds defeat.
In your shadow, I once felt the weight of your chain,
But now I rise, breaking free from your reign.
You built your fortress with whispers and fears,
Yet the strength in my heart has weathered the
years.
Each tear that I shed was a seed in the ground,
And from pain's bitter soil, my courage was found.
I'll dance in the light that you thought would be dim,
Unraveling all the doubts that you planted within.
For every insult, every scoff, every time you
dismissed,
Has forged a fierce spirit that can not be kissed.
The echoes of judgement may linger and swell,
But I've learned to embrace the strength in my shell.
Each flaw you pointed out, each laugh in my mind,
Is a brushstroke of beauty, uniquely designed.
Now watch as I flourish, as I break through
the night,
With every falter, I emerge into the light.
You're just a shadow, a flicker past,
While I'm the wildfire that's destined to last.
So here, in the ashes of what you believed,

I stand tall and proud, a soul now retrieved.
For no longer your victim, I'm ready to soar,
Watch me rise, watch me heal, I am so
much more!

145

River of Sacred Feeling

I bow to the tide that rises in my chest,
a holy current calling me home to rest.
No shield, no scold, no hurry to tame—
each trembling pulse I name without shame.
I cradle sorrow like rain on my skin,
let grief wash through me, thick and thin.
I breathe it gently, I breathe it deep,
a lantern for secrets my heart keeps.
Joy spills sunlight across the inner stream,
dancing on ripples of an answered dream.
I do not hoard, I do not flee—
I let it loosen, let it be free.
Anger is thunder, fierce and bright,
a clarion drum insists on the right.
I listen, I honor its clarifying flame,
Then softens the edges and soothes its name.
Fear is a shadow that asks to be seen;
I hold it kindly, not mean or clean.
Beneath its hush, courage quietly grows—
Roots of wisdom where compassion flows.
In this sacred current, I learn to belong,
each note of my heart a reverent song.
I am here, I am whole, I am learning to know
the grace of my tides as they come and they go.

She Is Worthy —
An Ode to the Quiet Flame

She is worthy of the ocean's patient light,
Of dawn that comes to heal the bruised night,
Worthy of hands that hold without a race,
Of whispered truths that honor every grace.
She is worthy of a hush that keeps her name,
Not spoken once for the trophy, but aflame
With reverence for the way her spirit bends
And mends the fragile edges life intends.
She is worthy of the kindness never brief,
Of someone steady in the storm of grief,
A shelter woven from a thousand days
Of listening to love in gentle ways.
She is worthy of a mirror that reflects
More than scars and more than lost

respect—

A mirror claiming value in her bone,
That says in the softest voice: you are

your own.

She is worthy of a slow morning, warm

and sure,

Of laughter that reminds her she's secure,
Of afternoons where time allows her

to breathe

To taste the small, defiant joy of depth.
She is worthy of a name that rings like home,
A room where courage learns again to roam,
Of arms that learn her history without shame,
And praise the courage that remains the same.

She is worthy of forgiveness, given whole,
Not bartered for performance, life, or soul,
For every fault she's carried like a stone
Deserves the grace to claim a softer tone.
She is worthy of a partner in the dark
Who keeps a lantern and believes in

her spark,

Who sees the constellations in her doubt
And maps a route until the stars come out.
She is worthy of a voice that sings her right,
Of words that drape her softly in the night,
A chorus that remembers how she stands,
Not one that measures worth with clumsy

hands

She is worthy of a life that knows her name
As a treasure, not a checklist to acclaim.
Of a space to fail, to rise, to fiercely dream,
to risk the edges of a boulder seam.
She is worthy of the slow, abundant trust
That grows in soil rooted deep, not just

in dust,

Worthy of honor, reverence, and truth,
A sacred keeping for her tender youth.
So lift her gently — let the world attend,
Let admiration be her faithful friend.
For every heartbeat echoing above
Keeps simple witness: she is worthy of love.

Snake pit

In the heart of the jungle, where shadows
dance with dread, lies a pit of serpents, their
scales glistening red.

Slithering silently, with eyes like polished
stones, they coil and constrict, their presence
unknown.

Beware the snake pit, a realm of ancient power,
where venom flows like rivers, and fear

becomes a flower.
Those who dare to venture into this
treacherous domain, are met with hissing
whispers, driving them insane.
But some are drawn to danger, compelled by
the unknown, seeking out the serpents in their

Kingdom of bone.

For in the depths of darkness, where the
serpents thieves, lies a hidden secret, waiting to
arrive.

And as you face the serpents, with courage in
your mind, remember that within you, a warrior
you will find.

For in the depths of danger, where the serpents
Sssway, lies the key to your destiny, awaiting the
light of day.

Speak Words Of Truth And Wisdom

Oh, speak the word of truth and wisdom
Let your voice cut through the noise
Guide us on the path to righteousness
With your words, we find our poise
For in the darkness of confusion
Your light will show the way
To lead us to a place of clarity
Where doubt and fear will stray
Speak of love and speak of courage
Of honor and of grace
For in your words, we find the strength
To stand firm in the face
Of trials and tribulations
That seeks to tear us down
Your wisdom is the beacon
That will never let us drown
So speak the words of truth and wisdom
Let it echo through the land
For in your voice, we find our solace
Guided by your hand.

Stay Positive and Do Your Best

In dawn's first light, let your heart ignite,
With hope shining brightly, erasing the night.
Believe in your power, let fear be your guest,
Keep moving forward, do your very best.
Through the storm and through the sunshine,

Stay steady, and stay true,

Each challenge, a lesson, a moment to renew.
Rise with the mornings, let courage attest,
For greatness lies in those who give their best.
Remember, your spirit is boundless and free,
Embrace every moment, let your dreams be the key.
Stay positive, shine, let your soul be blessed,
The world's yours to conquer - give it your best.
No mountain too high, no valley too deep,
With faith in your heart and the goals that you keep,
Every step forward is a chance to impress,
Believe in your journey, and do your very best.
In darkness, find your light, let your hope be your guide,
With kindness and courage walking by your side.
Your spirit is mighty, your soul can attest,
That joy comes to those who give their best.
So lift up your voice and speak with grace,

Embrace each moment, run your own race.
Stay positive, face every test,
Remember, in trying, you always do your best.

Teen Mother -Forced Abortion

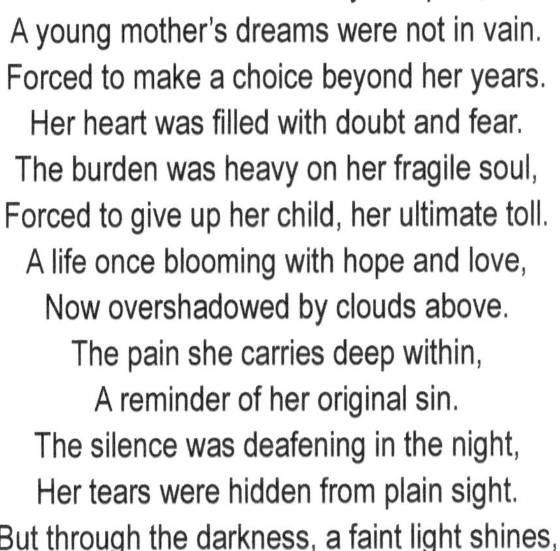

In a world of uncertainty and pain,
A young mother's dreams were not in vain.
Forced to make a choice beyond her years.
Her heart was filled with doubt and fear.
The burden was heavy on her fragile soul,
Forced to give up her child, her ultimate toll.
A life once blooming with hope and love,
Now overshadowed by clouds above.
The pain she carries deep within,
A reminder of her original sin.
The silence was deafening in the night,
Her tears were hidden from plain sight.
But through the darkness, a faint light shines,
A glimmer of hope in troubled times.
For though her road may be rough and steep,
She knows her love for her child runs deep.
So she stands tall, despite the pain,
Knowing her loss was not in vain.
For in her heart, her child will reside,
A love that will never subside.

Teen Pregnancy

In the bloom of youth, a life begins to grow,
A choice made in hastily, with consequences
to show.

The weight of responsibility, heavy on
tender shoulders,
As dreams of adolescence fade,
reality smolders.

Innocence lost in the shadow of an
unborn child,

The future's uncertain, emotions running wild.
Society judgment, whispers of shame,
A young mother's burden, her heart in flame.
But hope still flickers in the darkness of despair,
As new life stirs, a reason to care.
Through trials and tribulations, strength will
be found,

In the bond between mother and child, love
will abound.

So let us not judge, but extend a helping hand,

To guide the young parents, to help them stand.
For in the midst of struggle, seeds of resilience
are sown,

And from the depth of hardship, a beautiful
story is grown.

The Alchemy of a Single Heart

When dawn unfolds its quiet, golden seam,
We learn the world is softer than it seems.
A weary soul, once chained by naught but doubt,
Finds gates of grace where fear had shut
them out.
Not stars nor coins nor maps of fate's design
Could bind the path a lifted spirit finds;
For attitude, like prayer, can gently turn
Cold ash to ember, sorrow into burn.
A whispered yes, a courage newly dressed,
Transforms the heavy burden into rest.
What was once a storm becomes a teaching rain,
Each drop is a pulse that draws out dormant gain.
See kindness bloom where hardened edges stood,
And watch your shadow yield to tender good.
The future bends — a reed beneath your breath —
Not by fierce force, but by the peace you set.
So change, not hammered by a desperate plea,
But chosen like a slow, forgiven sea;
For inner light will steer the outward tide,
And altered thoughts will shape what waits outside.

Hold fast this truth: the soul's slight shift of view
Remakes the world, and makes the world renew.
The most significant discovery, quiet and true:
A changed heart writes a life both brave and new.

The Binary Shrine

We build a shrine of black and white, quick bricks of name and blame,
To paint the world in tidy strokes, and comfort our small flame.
It's easier to stamp a heart "good" or mark a face "bad."
Then stand inside the messy room where all our feelings are had.
A child of dusk and sunlight, each soul keeps both within —
A kindness like a lantern, a shadow like a sin.
We clap the seal and wear it, a label crisp and clean,
But labels hide the weather and the storms that lie between.
When anger drums its heartbeat, we call the person cruel.
When laughter breaks the morning, the same lips seem a jewel.
We dress the deed in verdicts, fast justice in our mind,
But mercy asks we linger, and tenderness to find,
For each harsh reaction, a secret might grow,
A wound that learned to armor so nobody could know.
For every gentle gesture, perhaps a debt is paid —
A memory that softened, a fear that softly swayed.
To hold another's shadow is to hold a trembling hand,
To know the thorn and the petal, both were planted
by the same land.
If you can bear the discord — the hunger, joy, and ache—
You learn the fragile grammar that two human hearts can make.
So when you feel the tremor of judgment rise and swell,
Pause like a river's eddy, listen to its bell.
Ask not, "Is this evil?" nor, "Is this saintly art?"

Ask, 'What storm or sunlight lives beneath this beating heart?"
Compassion is a workshop where we trade our rigid knives
For softer tools of language to carve the shapes of lives.
Forgiveness is not pardon for every hurtful thing,
But seeing why the wound was born and letting gentleness in.

It's holy work to handle the bouquet and the thorn,
To honor every season, the winter and the morn.
And when you stop dividing souls into good and bad,
You open doors to healing for the lost and for the sad.

So kneel before chaos, breathe in all the shades,
Accept the human symphony of laughter, fear, and rage.
For in the tender middle — where contradictions meet —
We learn the secret scripture: the world is whole, not neat.
Love asks us to be courageous to sit with what's unsure,
To let our heavy judgments soften, and let our hearts endure.
The altar of true insight is not clean lines or laws —
It's learning to hold otherness with reverence and because
Every person's orbit carries starlight strained by pain
Every angry morning can become a gentle rain.
And if you can embrace that truth, release the need to choose,
You'll find a wider heaven where forgiveness can infuse.
So name less, feel more deeply, let label fall away—
There is a better language that our kindred soul can say:
"I see you whole, complicit with your beauty and your scars,
I will not box your spirit — I will help unbar the bars."
For it's easier to call someone "bad" or "good," to close the door,"
But braver still to enter and to hear the thunder roar,
Be brave — be slow — be present — let your heart's wide harbor
stand,
And learn to keep both shadow and light within your hand

The Chosen Ones

In the whispers of the morning light,
They stir with purpose, pure and bright,
Guided by a sacred flame,
Destined to carry the sacred name.
Hearts of fire with love divine,
Paths aligned, a grand design,
Silent strength and gentle grace,
They move with purpose, time, and space.
Through shadows deep and stormy skies,
Their spirits rise, unbound, wise,
Bearing hope like sacred fire,
Lifting souls that do aspire.
The chosen ones, in unity, stand tall,
Answering heaven's silent call,
Bearing light in darkest night,
They are the dawn's eternal light.
May their journey be blessed and true,
With love eternal shining through,
The Chosen Ones, in spiritual grace,
Transform the world with boundless space.

The Dawn of Endeavors

And so the work begins, a journey, a quest,
With dreams afire, igniting the restless breast.
In the silence of dawn, where hopes softly rise,
We carve out our visions beneath open skies.
Each step is a promise, a whisper of fate,
Through struggles we wade, and through
triumphs we await.
Let doubts be but shadows, for light leads
the way
With courage as our armor, we sculpt a
new day.
In the tapestry woven with threads of the heart,
Resilience will flourish, and we shall not part.
For every endeavor, a lesson we glean
And with passion as fuel, we reignite
the unseen.
And so the work begins, with faith as our guide,
Together we'll soar. Hearts and hands
open wide.
Embrace every challenge, let your spirit ascend,
For within every journey, the magic transcends.

The Echoes of the Whole

I am the spark within the boundless sea,
A fleeting wave, then will flee.
I feel my edges, frame my small display,
a single breath that thinks it stands away.
Yet threads of starlight stitch my silent core,
A braided truth that knows we're less and more.
This optic veil - my mind's small, kindly ruse—
Makes "I" a lighthouse in the vast diffuse.
When sorrow folds and loneliness takes hold,
Remember: you are sunlight, warmth, and gold.
Each thought a ripple on the ocean's face ,
Each feeling-wind that moves through time and space.
Breathe deep; the hush will teach your heart to see:
You are the universe, through a brief degree.

The Harbor She Became

She walked through thunder, feet in shattered light,
learned how to count the stars in the darkest night.
Her hands were maps of storms she wouldn't hide,
turned every scar into proof of how she tried.
Where fear has splintered doors and broken beams,
She planted gardens grown from burned-out dreams.
Her laughter, iron tempered with soft gold,
a fortress, gentle, fierce, and brave and bold.
Men sought a legend whispered in the wind—
A strength unbroken, whole, where others thinned.
But she, who weathered tides and sharpened pain,
was not a prize to win, but hope to reign.
She is the harbor, steady, wide, and true—
The strength they dream of finding, born anew.

The Keeper

In the heart of the forest deep,
Where ancient secrets silently keep,
There dwells a keeper wise and old,
Whose stories of history unfold.
With eyes that see beyond the veil,
He guards the truth; he will not fail.
Through trials and tribulations untold,
He stands strong, a fortress bold.
His hands are calloused, his spirit unbroken.
From dusk 'til dawn, his vigil unspoken.
The keeper of the forest's lore,
A guardian of what came before.
In shadows cast by moonlight's glow,
He walks amidst the whispering boughs.
His presence is a beacon in the night,
Guiding lost souls toward the light.
Oh, keeper of the ancient wood,
In your wisdom, we find all good.
Protect us from the darkest deep,
And in your care, our souls will keep.

The Lament of Humanity

In shadows deep, where hopes
once gleamed,
A river flows, silent and unseen,
Tears shed for the souls betrayed,
For dreams unmet, for love delayed.
O human race, in your heart's abyss,
Lies, pain, despair, a silent hiss,
Yet in weeping, sparks ignite,
A beacon born from the darkest night.
Each tear a story, a silent cry,
Of innocence lost, and the fallen sky,
Of kindness buried under disdain,
Of hope rising through pain.
We mourn not merely what's been torn,
But what we've yearned to be reborn,
In every tear, a hope persists,
A plea for peace that still exists.
Let tears become the seed of change,
The cradle of a world rearranged,
For in our sorrow, strength is found,
And in our mourning, love is bound.
Rise, O spirit, from the rain,
Transform the tears into refrain—
A song of hope, a call for grace,

Revive the humane aspect of the

Human Race.

The Quiet Harbor

She gathers lightning in the palms of night,
Turns jagged thunder into softened light;
Where gale and grief would crack a weaker bone,
She stands—an ember steady, all her own.
Her eyes have learned to map each bitter storm,
To braid the winds, to keep some warmth from harm;
When ruins whisper that the heart is done,
She plants new songs and teaches the dawn to run.
Her beauty is the bridge she builds from pain,
A ribbon mended after every strain;
She gives her heart like rain that finds the earth,
Unfazed by what the past declared of worth.
She wears her scars like constellations bright,
Each marks a story carved from endless night;
They map the miles she walked through fear
and flame,
A quiet testament that time can't tame.
Her laughter is a lighthouse after the wreck,
A steady beam when all the ropes came
unchecked;
She offered mercy seasoned by her strife,
A soft, unyielding architecture of life.
Not fragile—fortress, woven out of care,
A tender armor born from all despair;

And when she loves, it's gravity refined,
a force that steadies drifting, the fractured mind.
So praise the hands that heal what storms erase—
The gentle force that gives the human race.
So honor not the surface, but the soul:

The one who bends the world back toward
the whole.

The Quiet Muscle

When barbs are thrown like weather, sharp
and loud,
And voices rises to claim the higher ground,
I feel a furnace flicker in my chest —
A small revolt that will not let me rest.
The world insists that fury proves my worth,
But rage is thunder circling its own hurt.
So breathe slow, and teach my hands to stay,
To fold the knives of the answer back away.
There is a courage not in roaring flame
But in the steady keeping of my name;
A patient pulse that does not bargain cheep
With honor lost in echoes others keep.
Respect, they say, is earned — yet sudden

sneers

Can make a mirror fog with sudden tears.
I learn to hold my dignity like stone,
Not brittle glass smashed by a passing tone.
I practice quiet as if forging steel,
Each measure pauses a strike, each calm a seal.
The absence of a shout does not mean less —
It is a different kind of wilderness:

A field where silence trains a softer spine,
Where margins set by self are by design .
Not apathy, nor fear, nor turning blind;
But choosing peace when storms would curl

the mind.

When disrespect comes wearing careless clothes,
I greet it like the weather, watch it close.
I let the words go by like leaves in stream,
Reserve my answer for my truer dreams.

Sometimes I speak — but not to feed the flame —
I speak to teach, to heal, to name the name.
Sometimes I walk — and in the walking know
That dignity can grow where tempers bow.
This growth is hidden in a quieter plot,
A tender muscle learning where it's not
Obligated to match the volume of a shout —
To win by staying whole, not lashing out.
One day, I wake and find my ruin mended:
The breath, the pause, the peace — my heart

befriended.

And in that calm, I find a fiercer you:
A self that stands, unbroken, honest, true.

The Rise in Every Fall

In shadows deep where doubts reside,
And trembling hearts seek strength to hide,
There whispers a truth so bold and clear,
A voice that calms the trembling fear.
The journey's fraught with stumbles and pain,
Each failure leaves its haunting stain,
But pause, and hear this silent call—
True strength is rising, after all.
For the fallen souls may doubt their light,
Yet dawn returns to chase the night,
And in each fall, a lesson lies,
A spark to ignite new skies.
No champion's story is complete,
Without the scars and the bittersweet,
For every fall's a step to grow,
A chance to stand, to learn, to show.
So, weary heart, embrace the fall,
For in your rise, you conquer all,
The path is ours, both brave and true,
Every fall, strength waits for you.

The Unbound Wings

In a world where shadows cast
their sway,
She rose from whispers of yesterday.
no longer bound by chains unseen,
Her spirit soared, untamed, serene.
Once she shrank to fit the mold,
In silent rooms, her stories untold.
But now a force, a radiant light,
She spreads her wings and takes
fearless flight.

Her voice was a storm, a breaking
tide,
No longer quiet, nor pushed aside.
In her heart, a fire ignites,
A beacon against the timid nights.
Daring dreams once held in stealth,
Now unfurl into their fullest wealth.
With every step, she carves her space,
A dance of power, a bolder trace.
Unfettered by the world's confines,
She writes new tales in untamed lines.
Embrace her strength, the path she
paves,

In bright defiance, she no longer craves.
From whispers past to roaring seas,
She stands unbound,- infinite, and free.

Trust In Yourself

In the depths of uncertainty, trust in yourself
shines bright,
A beacon of strength, guiding you through the
darkest night.
Believe in your worth, in your power to prevail,
For in your own courage, you shall never fail.
Embrace the fire within, let it fuel your
every step,
With unwavering determination, you shall
never forget.
Trust in your instincts, in the wisdom of
your heart,
For in your own truth, you shall find a
fresh start.
In the face of doubt, stand tall and stand firm,
For in your own convictions, you shall
always affirm.
Have faith in your journey, in the path
you tread,
For in your own spirit, you shall never be led.
Trust in yourself, in the strength that lies within,
For in your own essence, you shall surely win.
Let go of fear, embrace the power you possess,
For in yourself, you shall always find success.

Uncover The Truth

In the shadows deep, the secrets lie,
But truth prevails; it cannot hide.
Uncover now, the veils of lies,
And let the light illuminate our eyes.
For falsehoods may deceive and sway,
But honesty will find its way.
The path of truth is clear and bright,
Guiding us through the darkest night.
No longer shall we live in doubt,
The truth revealed, we will devout.
Uncover Now, the hidden schemes,
And let us see beyond the dreams.
For in the depths of lies and fear,
The truth will always persevere.
So let us seek it out with might,
And bask in its revealing light.
Uncover now, the mysteries untold,
And let the truth forever hold.
In every heart, in every mind,
The power of truth we shall find.

Vibrant Spirit, Purposeful Heart

In the dawn of each new day, I rise with the sun,
My energy's vibrant, my journey's just begun.
With every heartbeat echoing a rhythm so true,
I dance through the moments, embracing the hue.
Color of passion, of strength, and of grace,
Illuminate pathways, revealing my place.
With purpose as my compass, I navigate the tide,
Through valleys of challenge, I boldly will stride.
With laughter as my armor and dreams as my guide,
I soar through the skies, with the universe wide.
Each step is a manifestation of visions I hold,
A tapestry woven with threads of pure gold.
For hope is my anchor, and love is my light,
In the depths of the darkness, I shine ever bright.
When shadows may whisper doubt in my ear,
I rise up in defiance, dispelling all fear.
I embrace every tear as a lesson, a sigh,
For in moments of struggle, my spirit will fly.
With each experience, my essence grows strong,
I find strength in the struggle; I sing my own song.
So here's to the journey, the highs and the lows,
The beauty of living, where growth truly flows.
My energy's vibrant, my spirit's alive,
With purpose ignited, I flourish and thrive.

When Shadows Rise and Whispers Regret

When shadows rise and whisper
regret,

A hush of dusk where prayers
are met,

The heart unfolds its secret ache,
Like lanterns dim on twilight's lake.
Each echo bears a lesson burned,
A soul's refrain for paths unturned,
Regret, a teacher wrapped in pain,
Transforms the loss to sacred gain.
Beneath the moon's imperial eye,
Old vows dissolve, new truths reply,
We sift the ash of choices made,
And find that grace is softly laid.
Kneel low, breathe in the starlit debt,
Forgiveness grows where we beget
A humble offering — tear and plea —
That frees the self to simply be.
So let the shadows speak their
name,

Not chains of shame but kindled
flame,

Their whisper guides — a quiet net
To catch the soul from deep regret.

When Someone Says no: It's No!!!

When someone says no, it's No!
Respect their choice, let them go
No means stop, no means wait
Listen to their words, don't debate
No is a boundary, set in place
A clear message: don't try to erase
It's a sign of strength and self-respect
To honor it is an actual act of grace
No is powerful, no is firm
It's not a request, no room to squirm
So when someone tells you no
Take a step back, let it show
No is a declaration, not up for negotiation
A simple statement, with no hesitation
So when you hear those two letters spoken
Remember, when someone says no, it's No!!!

Whispers Unveiled

In a shadow deep, where silence dwells,
A secret blooms, as twilight swells.
Veiled in whispers, it danced discreet,
Yet now it rises on unsteady feet.
With every glance, the truth takes flight,
Revealed beneath the silver light.
A tapestry woven of dreams and fears,
Now laid bare, transcending years.
No longer cloaked in shades of night,
The echoes of trust ignite the light.
In the corridors of thoughts confined,
A revelation, both cruel and kind.
From hushed confessions to roaring tides,
The heart's own secrets no longer bides.
Each word, a spark; each silence, a gale,
As honesty weaves its intricate trail.
Yet in this unmasking, we find our grace,
For in vulnerability, we embrace our place.
The world shall witness, with bated breath,
The beauty of truth, even in death.
So let the shadows retreat from the dawn,
As we stand in the light, reborn and drawn.
For every secret that slips from its shroud,
Transform us anew, in truth, we are proud.

Wings of Defiance

In shadows deep where doubts conspire,
Your words ignited a burning fire.
"You'll never rise," the critics said,
But from your doubt, my dreams were bred.
I'll climb the mountains, pierce the skies,
With every step, my spirit flies.
Each whispered fear, a gust of wind,
Propelling me where hope begins.
With wings of courage, I'll take my flight,
Through storms and trials, I'll find my light.
Your doubt, a chain, I'll break apart,
As I chase the dreams that fill my heart.
For when you said I couldn't go,
I found the strength to boldly grow.
I'll rise like the sun upon the morn,
Transcending limits, reborn, adorned.
With every heartbeat, I choose to soar,
To reach the heights, unlock the door.
So here I stand, against the tide,
An anthem strong, I will abide.
In every challenge, I find my way,
Your doubt, a spark to fuel my stay.
For those who doubt, I'll gently prove,
With wings of defiance, I shall move.

So watch me soar, watch me ascend,
A testament that dreams can mend.
I'll rise above, with heart so true,
All because you said I couldn't do.

Women, Treat Your Man Like a King

In the heart of the home, where love finds its way,
With kindness and respect, let your spirits sway.
Treat him like royalty, let your heart collide.
A king needs a queen, not just on a throne,
But in laughter and struggles, together they've grown.
With grace in your actions and warmth in your voice,
You build a strong bond, give each other a choice.
When he treats you like treasure, with honor and care,
Return the affection and let your love be rare.
For love is a dance, a rhythm divine,
In the steps that you take, let your souls intertwine.
Respect him, uplift him, in all that you do,
For love that is nurtured can flourish anew.
Support his ambitions, let dreams take their flight,
With faith in each other, you'll conquer the night.
In times that are stormy, when shadows may loom,
Stand firm by his side, let your heart be the room.
A king's greatest strength comes from love that you give,
In the light of your trust, together you'll live.
So cherish each moment, let gratitude sing,
For love that is balanced, is a powerful thing.
Women, treat your man as a king, strong and true,
As long as he treats you like the queen that you grew.

You Are Chosen to be Awakened by God

In the quiet dawn of your soul's deep night,
A whisper echoes softly, shining bright.
Gentle hands of grace, divine and true,
Have marked a time for awakening—

especially for you.

He chose your heart to feel His sacred fire,
To lift you higher, to lift you higher.
A mission woven in the threads of your fate,
To shine His light, to love, to consecrate.
Rise now from the shadows, step into the
morning's grace,

The world awaits your courage, your
tender embrace.

For you are chosen, a vessel of divine song,
Born to awaken, to make the broken strong.
With every breath, remember, you are His plan,
A beacon of hope in this vast land.
Hold firm to His call, let faith be your guide—
You are chosen to awaken, with God by

Your side.

You Do Not Walk Alone

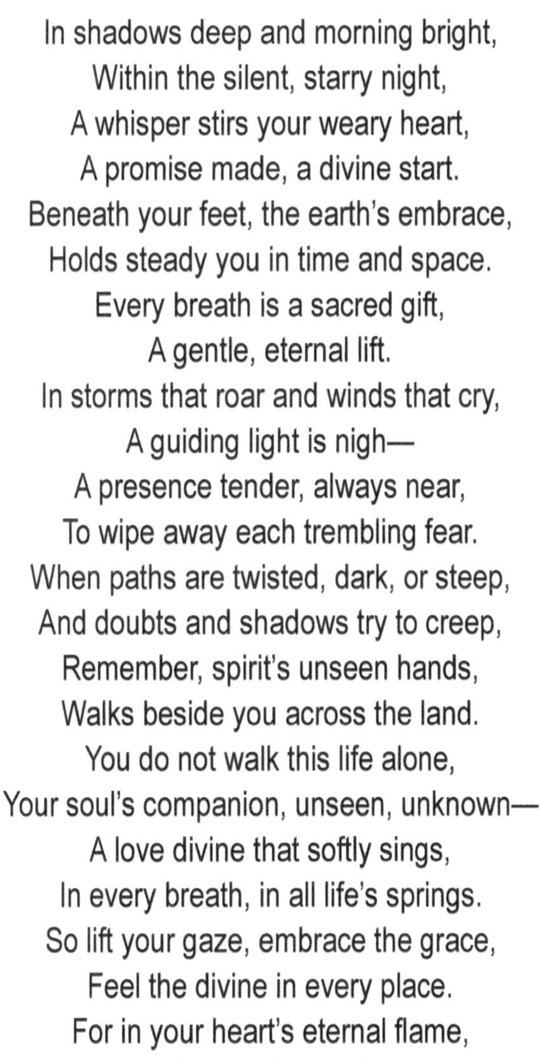

In shadows deep and morning bright,
Within the silent, starry night,
A whisper stirs your weary heart,
A promise made, a divine start.
Beneath your feet, the earth's embrace,
Holds steady you in time and space.
Every breath is a sacred gift,
A gentle, eternal lift.
In storms that roar and winds that cry,
A guiding light is nigh—
A presence tender, always near,
To wipe away each trembling fear.
When paths are twisted, dark, or steep,
And doubts and shadows try to creep,
Remember, spirit's unseen hands,
Walks beside you across the land.
You do not walk this life alone,
Your soul's companion, unseen, unknown—
A love divine that softly sings,
In every breath, in all life's springs.
So lift your gaze, embrace the grace,
Feel the divine in every place.
For in your heart's eternal flame,
You are forever loved, the same

You Said "I Look Like A Beached Whale."

In the vast expanse where the ocean meets
the land,

A cruel remark left me feeling unmanned.
"You look like a beached whale," the words
did impart,

A wound to my soul, a dagger to my heart.
But do not be fooled by the hurtful disdain,
For beneath the surface, true beauty remains.
A creature of grace, of strength, and of might,
A symbol of power, of resilience in spite.
I may resemble a whale on shore,
But within me lies so much more.
For beauty is not just skin deep, you see,
It's the spirit within that truly sets me free.
So don't judge me by my appearance alone,
For I am more than just flesh and bone.
I am a force to be reckoned with, a sight,
to behold,

Despite your words that left me cold.
So let me rise up from the sands, strong and tall,
For I am not just a beached whale after all.

You Thought I Would Lie Down And Die

In the face of adversity, I stood tall and strong
Defying the odds, proving them all wrong
Though they thought I would crumble and fall
I rose up triumphant, standing proud and tall
They thought I would lie down and die
But I refused to yield, to surrender,

or comply

For deep within me burns a fierce fire
A determination that will never tire
I may stumble, I may falter
But I will never be defeated, never alter
My resolve is unwavering, my spirit

indomitable

I will rise above, I will be unstoppable
So do not underestimate me, do not count
me out

For I am a force to be reckoned with, without
a doubt

Though they thought I would lie down and die
I am a survivor, I will always defy.